SEX

The Masterpiece of Happines

ARLINDO FERNANDES

SEX
THE MASTERPIECE OF HAPPINES

iUniverse books may be ordered through booksellers or by contacting:

iUniverse
1663 Liberty Drive
Bloomington, IN 47403
www.iuniverse.com
844-349-9409

ISBN: 978-1-6632-5640-9 (sc)
ISBN: 978-1-6632-5641-6 (e)

Library of Congress Control Number: 2023917654

Print information available on the last page.

iUniverse rev. date: 02/16/2024

Disclaimer

This guidebook is designed to provide information on sex. The author is not offering medical or technical advice. The author and publisher deny any responsibility for any loss or damage allegedly caused by this book.

Contents

Introduction

The circumstances by which we originated don't matter. What matters is that the process evolved with love, care, and desire, all for the purpose of filling the obligation of the mystery of the incomprehensible, while never understanding with certainty how it happened in the way it happened or how it will end. We do have some certainty that in the five- to seven-day marathon of many competitors—up to two hundred sperm compete—only the one that penetrates first will fertilize the egg. And that proves that each of us is a winner from the very beginning.

Winning the marathon is the first step of the long, complicated, and mysterious process of transforming a tiny, thick, whitish liquid into something extraordinarily amazing and complicated. There is a time limit for complete development, for which we must wait, to truly become one; otherwise, we are a winner who didn't make the cut. We can't temper with time, even if we wanted to. Seven months, minimum—preferably nine—are necessary to get us ready to experience what we are meant to be. The only thing we can do is hope that everything goes the way it is supposed to go during that period, so we can count as the desired and wished-for ones.

I believe that while we impatiently wait, we imagine the world of even greater astonishment. It has to be so wonderful, the true paradise for us to enjoy from one beginning to the other end. We can almost smell, feel, see, and touch that paradise. We must be special, and what awaits us must match what we are. And as much as we want to break free and begin the new journey in that paradise, the desire of others, especially our moms and dads, is equal to ours, to welcome us to the paradise. We make them look and feel even more special. We give them confidence that they have reached the expected milestone—and gone beyond. If we are the firstborn, the joy of satisfaction is elevated.

Now that we are free, part two of life begins. We are winners, heroes at birth, born for continuity and difference. We carry the torches of hope and prosperity of those before us, for us, and to those after us. Because we are winners—heroes with specialties—much is expected of us, and deliverance becomes our obligation. Our heroism and specialty include astonishing development in phases (insemination, gamete, zygote, embryo, fetus, baby, infant, preadolescence, adolescence, emerging and early adulthood, young adult, adult, old adult, and death). From these rises an interesting game that involves passion, love, affection, and desires (relationship), with the utmost bewildering trophy—sex. We receive training, guidance, and support to help us stand on our feet and grasp the necessary means to fulfill the dreams of so many by accomplishment of our mission. Thus, failure is not acceptable. We are the ones with great powers. "With great power comes great responsibility." Responsibility encompasses our total and unconditional commitment to a successful sexual journey.

Puberty

Puberty is the process of physical and physiological changes in which a child's body becomes capable of sexual procreation. It is triggered by hormonal signals from the brain to the gonads—reproductive glands, such as ovaries and testicles. In response to the signals, the gonads produce hormones that stimulate libido as well as the growth, function, and transformation of the hair, skin, breasts, muscle, bones, sex organs, and brain. The external sex organs (primary sexual characteristics) distinguish boys from girls, and puberty leads to secondary characteristics that further differentiate boys from girls. These gradual but drastic changes in youth explain the complexity and difficulties of puberty, with the following milestones:

- Gonadarche at age eight, the earliest gonadal (ovaries, and testis) changes
- Adrenarche at age eleven, an early stage in sexual maturation that peaks at around twenty years of age

- Thelarche, or breast budding, at age eleven in females; the start of secondary breast development, where boys' and girls' breasts differentiate due to variance in hormone levels
- Pubarche at age twelve; the appearance of pubic hair
- Menarche at age 12.5; first menstruation
- Spermarche at age 13.5; first ejaculation

Two significant differences between puberty in girls and that in boys are the age at which puberty begins and the major sex steroids involved—the androgen (a male sex organ such as testosterone) and the estrogen. Despite a wide range of normal ages, puberty in girls starts at ages ten to eleven and ends at ages fifteen to seventeen. In boys, it begins at ages eleven to twelve. The major landmark of puberty for girls is menarche, which occurs, on average, between ages twelve and thirteen; for boys, it is spermarche or first ejaculation, which occurs at age thirteen.

In the twenty-first century, the average age at which youth, especially girls, reach specific signs of puberty was lower than in the nineteenth century, where the age was fifteen for girls and seventeen for boys. This could be due to many factors, including improved nutrition. On the other hand, environmental conditions, such as poverty, poor nutrition, and pollution can delay puberty. Puberty that starts earlier is known as precocious puberty, and puberty that starts later is known as delayed puberty.

❑ Effects of Precocious and Delayed Puberty

Several studies have found that the outcomes of early puberty in girls can be psychologically damaging. The main issue is physical development. Early-maturing girls can develop a negative view of their body images for many reasons, including teasing from peers about their visible breasts, which may force them to hide their breasts by dressing differently. These experiences lead to lower self-esteem, depression, and social isolation. Also, as physical and emotional differences set them apart from peers, early-maturing girls develop relationships with older boys or even have older boyfriends, who are attracted to the girls with women's physiques and girlish innocence. Having an older boyfriend could improve popularity among peers, but the negative side effects could be risky and unlawful behaviors, including alcohol and drug use and abuse and underage and unprotected sex. Each alone is potentially capable of harming girls' futures; combined, these could destroy their lives. By contrast, later puberty in girls brings positive behaviors in adolescence that continue to adulthood.

Early puberty in boys has been linked with positive outcomes, such as popularity among peers, higher self-esteem, and self-confidence because of physical developments—greater height, developed muscles, and athletic abilities—leading to leadership in high school and success in adulthood. Recent studies, however, have shown that problems might outweigh the benefits, as teenage boys are more prone to risky behaviors and aggressiveness, leading to increased sexual activity, teenage pregnancy, anger toward parents, and disobedience to authorities, which can trigger depression and other psychosocial issues.

Contrary to late-maturing girls, late-maturing boys face negative outcomes that include being unpopular among peers due to their poorly developed physiques, antisocial sentiment, low self-confidence and self-esteem, and more anxiety; they also are more afraid of intimacy and sexual activities than other boys.

Clearly, early and late puberty carry consequences, but so does life. Unless you are extremely early or extremely late, the timing of your puberty should not affect your future. Also, every individual is a unique human being. Whatever happened to your friends at a certain age won't necessarily happen to you. Care about the phenomena that raise immediate concerns for you.

❑ Changes

In boys, puberty begins with the enlargement of the testicles and scrotum and the development of pubic hair. Their testicles begin making sperm, and the penis becomes able to ejaculate semen. Their first ejaculation occurs at age thirteen. Ejaculations can occur during sleep, called nocturnal emission, which continues throughout their lifespans as biological sexual maintenance or when a long period has passed without having sex.

By the end of puberty, boys (now young men) have heavier bones and almost twice as much muscle. Some of the bone growth (shoulder width and jaw) is great and differentiates male from female physiques. The average adult male can have up to three times more lean body mass than a female and about half the body fat. This muscle growth develops mainly in the later stages of puberty and progresses well into adulthood.

Erections. Erections can occur spontaneously at any time of day. When boys reach their teenage years, erections occur more frequently, and they experience *nocturnal penile tumescence*, or erections that happen during sleep or waking up, colloquially called *morning hood*. I believe this is part of the natural process of readiness for fatherhood.

The first physical sign of puberty in girls is usually a firm, tender lump under the center of the breasts at about ten years of age. Within six to twelve months, the swelling visibly extends beyond the edges of the areola. This is stage three of breast development, which continues to stage five.

Vagina, uterus, and ovaries. Perineal skin changes as estrogen increases its resistance to infections. The mucosal surface of the vagina becomes thicker and pink (in contrast to the brighter red of the prepubertal vaginal mucosa). Estrogen increases glycogen content in the vaginal epithelium, which will play an important role in maintaining vaginal pH and the normal whitish vaginal secretions. The uterus and ovaries increase in size during the two years following thelarche, or breasts development.

Menstrual fertility. This happens between ages twelve and thirteen (earlier for some and later for others; anytime between eight and sixteen is considered normal). Ovulation, the necessary occurrence for fertility, in general, doesn't accompany the earliest menstruation but can happen. Therefore, consider pregnancy on top of all possible tragedies or sour fruits in teenage sexual activities.

Body odor and acne. The rising levels of androgens can change the fatty-acid composition of perspiration into adult body odor and increase the odds for acne, a skin condition that is very characteristic of puberty and varies in severity in both boys and girls.

Puberty is a bewildering biological roller coaster that every human being will ride. It's one of the most important milestones for everyone. Yet numerous adults have endured a hard-life battle in adulthood because of their untamed puberty, where the main culprits were disrespect for laws and authority, becoming teen parents, drugs and alcohol abuse, and thefts and other crimes.

Puberty can make you or destroy you. Respecting your physical and physiological changes, obedience to and cooperation with mature adults, and knowledge of puberty's intricacies are the must-be-honored requirements for your successful life, which includes education, integrity, wealth, and prosperity. All will lead you to a very successful sexual journey.

The Power of a Kiss

There is more than one theory on how kissing originated and why we do it. Some scientists believe kissing is a learned behavior, as roughly 10 percent of humans don't kiss. Others believe kissing is instinctual. Because other animals—birds, fish, bonobos, and chimpanzees (our closest ancient ancestors)—kiss, I believe kissing is an instinctual, rather than a learned, behavior. Ten percent doesn't make it a rule. Besides, poor use or no use of a skill doesn't mean lack of natural abilities. Indoor cats suck at hunting and might not eat their prey, but their poor or great abilities to hunt never dies.

Regardless of accords or disagreements about the origin of kissing, there are many types of kisses. Their importance may vary with person, culture, tradition, myths, and misconceptions, and—except Jesus Christ—kissing is beneficial to all.

❑ Types of Kissing

Betrayal kiss. Public information says that the kiss of Judas, or the betrayal of Christ, is the act in which Judas identified Jesus to the multitude who had come from the chief priest and elders of the people to arrest him. The kiss that Judas gave led to Jesus's arrest by the police force of the Sanhedrin (the highest court of justice and the supreme council in ancient Jerusalem) and his subsequent execution.

Peace kiss. Also called the holy kiss or the brother/sister kiss, this is an ancient traditional Christian greeting that signifies a wish and blessing that peace be with the recipient. This kiss was also shared among apostles before their martyrdom.

Social ritual kiss. Kissing is a social ritual almost worldwide. Kissing friends' cheeks is a standard greeting in many countries and cultures. In Europe and Latin America, people kiss the cheeks of family, friends, and even someone to whom they're introduced as a greeting or a show of respect, appreciation, or congratulations. The number of kisses varies from one to three, depending on the occasion and meaning.

In some cultures, women kiss men and other women, but it's unpopular for men to kiss other men who are not family or close friends. Instead, they shake hands. Countries where men kiss each other include:

- Argentine
- Belgium

- Chile
- Italy
- France
- Netherlands
- Spain
- Uruguay

Bonding kiss. Children feel special when they are kissed, especially by their parents, family members, and people they admire. Its meaning—affection, love, care, and admiration—is doubled when a hug follows the kiss.

Emotional kiss. Parents and family members kiss their sons and daughters when they win a competition that had high expectations. Soccer players are famous for kissing each other after a goal and winning the match.

Achievement kiss. The long tradition of "trophy kissing" is another way to express happiness, joy, and pride.

Personal or love kiss. Some soccer players kiss their wrist tattoos or rings on their fingers, for example, to say "I love you" to their significant ones. (Former players Raúl González and Rivaldo, are examples.) Women always give an "I love you too" kiss to their lovers after receiving jewelry and gifts. If you haven't gotten a sweet kiss after her intense orgasm, be patient. It will come to you, too.

Commitment kiss. While the history of kissing the bride is ambiguous, it seems that the tradition began in ancient Rome. Marriage was (and still is, as it should be!) seen as a contract signed by a kiss. That's why, for the longest time, after the words "Until death do us part," we hear "You may kiss the bride." It's the reason "sealed with a kiss" is popular. And here comes the heart of the matter: erotic kisses.

❏ Erotic Kisses

The first kiss. Social norms and misconceptions make us assume the first kiss is a tormenting endeavor, a must-pass exam or you're a loser. This is a crazy proposal that spoils the fun. First kiss is the first day at the kindergarten of pleasure. It doesn't matter how much we know; our first day is about fun, joy, and happiness, not winning a certificate of excellence. We might remember this day for a very long time or even forever because it's an extraordinary event, which means we should ease ourselves into it instead of losing sleep over it.

The more you know what to expect with the first kiss, the greater your eagerness and readiness to have it, but practice only will give you an idea of when and how to lead or follow a kiss. And then, it will be great and effortless. Therefore, whether you or your lover has kissed before or both haven't, keeping a low expectation lowers the pressure and increases the odds of satisfaction. More importantly, talk about what you expect to learn and do on your fist kiss beforehand. Reassure each other that your first kiss is not a test. It will be a memorable experience between two individuals in love.

Plan a day for it. Go on a date—any activity that allows fun, relaxation, and dialogue. Talk about the upcoming kiss without dwelling on it to avoid worries. "I can't wait to kiss those beautiful lips tonight" could be enough of talking about it. Only you know what can put you in a mood for the first kiss and how you want to do it.

Women, when the moment of truth comes, briefly send him an I-am-ready message and kiss his lips softly. He should respond in kind, sending you a message that says, "Thank you, God, I can hardly resist it any longer. Let's feel each other's souls."

Men, once the mood is aroused by touch or caress, for example, whether comfortably seated or standing, start your journey with a soft kiss on the neck—not too wet, not too soft, just right for her. Move to the lips for two or three mutual kisses. Suck on her lower lip, then the top. Kiss the other side of her neck and return to the lips. Repeat and add variety.

Play with your tongue between her lips. This is a nice request for tongue play. She could voluntarily do this move. Go on sucking gently on each other's tongue tips. Circle the tongue; do whatever feels pleasurable. Consider using your hands to touch and caress the other erogenous zones to increase the sexual pleasure of the kissing. You can go as far as inserting fingers inside her and make some gentle moves, including stroking her vagina, but control your emotion as pleasure intensifies. An aggressive kiss is not necessarily more pleasurable, nor does it prove that you're a good kisser. Gentle is always the best way with women.

Be humble and relaxed, and enjoy it. To take a breath, hold your lips against hers, or break the kiss, fill your lungs, and release. Do not let negative thoughts bother you. Simply enjoy what you're doing. Just the lip contact is a memorable experience, but continue pouring honey into the mug for a cup of delicious tea. You've got nothing to lose! If your lover dumps you because your kissing sucks, he or she has saved you from relationship's hurdle out of ignorance. And they will never know what they missed. Indulge in your first kiss without bias.

If kissing is all that is today, beware of redirecting the main source of pleasure. When you reach her vulva, her most powerful erogenous zone, and play with her vagina or clitoris sufficiently, the pleasure coming from her vulva overtakes that of her kiss. Therefore, once you realize the kissing has reached its climax, end the session by reversing the moves to the starting point; decrease the intensity of the kisses gradually. A final gentle kiss on the lips seals the deal. If you desire more, take a quick break and start over. This time, linger on whatever was more pleasurable before. End the kiss same way as before.

It's very unlikely to hit a double jackpot in one event— first kiss, and the first sex act, whether oral or penetrative— but when sex follows your first kiss, don't be afraid to stimulate all erogenous zones, especially the vulva. Just do not rush to sex, or you didn't give the first kiss all it deserves. As your first kiss is also foreplay, don't end it by reversing to the starting point. Follow the rules of pleasure, and use your imagination for great sex. Don't let anyone fool you that your first kiss, alone or followed by sex, will be your greatest ever. Unless you are mature and sufficiently knowledgeable about sex, abstain from further sexual activities on your first kiss.

First French kiss. French kissing someone for the first time shouldn't be as worrying as the first kiss. Experience is on our sides; we know the best places for our hands and how to avoid the awkwardness of certain positions and how to avoid bumping heads. Yet this could be our worst enemy because experience gives us confidence, but confidence works best with comfort, and comfort is built on repetition. The first French kiss with someone can't be the greatest because, despite your experience, you are exploring each other's pleasure. Like the first kiss, the first French kiss is an examination.

Remember that kissing is a sexual journey, demanding body, mind, and spirit participation. If you approach it with a testing attitude, you automatically invite the devil to join the party. Be relaxed, go with the flow, and enjoy the ride. Feel free to laugh at silly moves, such as bumping heads. Be gentle, patient, and appreciative. Why spoil the fun?

The intense desire to kiss someone for the first time can elevate pleasure and fool us into believing we got the jackpot on the first attempt. Since we don't experience pleasure in the same way as others, someone may not like his or her hair, back, or buttocks caressed during kissing but will fake pleasure to keep the momentum going. Talking about kissing beforehand clears the road for a smooth ride all the way to paradise.

Surveys say that to some women, kissing can make or break their partners' chances of getting to their downtown. Misconception, too, says that a good job with the upper lips opens the bottom lips—these are different ways to say that if you are a bad kisser, you can forget about getting to her vagina. Those who live by that philosophy are trapped because a stumble at the door doesn't kill the possibilities of making a great entry into the house. Your poor performance on the first try doesn't mean you can't improve and become a star.

You also have heard that love is blind. That's true! When you like or love someone, your heart tricks your mind in judgment. Everything in that person is uniquely beautiful. All their actions seem great, passionate, and better than anyone else's. Their touches are tantalizing, and their kisses are the most pleasurable you've ever had. When you take them inside you, you become a different person. They have discovered pleasure buttons you didn't know you had. You can hardly wait to feel that again. And then, everything starts to cool off. The true character emerges. His kisses are still pleasurable but not as much anymore. His penis is fine, and the sex is good but not so great anymore. His flaws are no longer protected by the power of your passion; rather, they are revealed by the superiority of your brain.

You've just realized that your heart trapped you, and his first kisses fooled you. The first impression is not necessarily the reflection of the whole.

If a kiss determines whether you will have sex with someone, you could be judged as a cheap woman, one who shows a poor understanding of relationship development. You could lose a potential lover. Any individual can become a great kisser, and any woman can turn a horrible kisser into a great one. If he's a great kisser but horrible at exploring your vulva or doesn't respect you and place your satisfaction first, you lose out tremendously.

Similar to the first kiss, French kissing someone for the first time isn't always the greatest, simply because what's pleasurable for one person may be unpleasant for another. You don't know what moves will bring the most pleasure to the one you're kissing. Also, anxiety and concern can get in the way of relaxation and enjoyment.

You can give natural feedback during a kiss, but an honest assessment of this journey is best achieved by communication. It helps you understand each other and enjoy kissing in a way that's pleasurable for both of you. The misconceptions around the first kiss and first French kiss make us shy away from talking about them beforehand. Don't follow this nonsense. Remember, the more we know a person, the better our ability to please him or her. Communication is a key factor in human relations; it's fundamental in relationships, and it's a must in the first kiss and kissing someone for first time. Here's a communication sample:

> "I really liked it when you _____"
> "_____ felt really good, too."
> "I wanna do more [or less] of _____ next time."
> "Did you like it when I _____? What about _____?"
> "_____ doesn't do much for me. Just so you know, especially if it does for you."
> "I heard about _____. Can we try it next time?"

The foreplay kisses. It seems that the world is spinning faster; "time flies" is real. We've become creatures with many daily tasks. We rush everything we do, even in bed. (In fact, I'm writing this chapter in a rush!) How sad, but it's not tragic, and you don't have to be a victim. Sex is the greatest pleasure to humankind. Foreplay is the first step of this adventure. Kissing and touching are the two elements of foreplay. Even though you can skip foreplay (although not recommended), when you cut to the chase, you haven't taken the time to get all the pleasure of kissing before you move to the next phase of your sexual journey. You've cheated. You already know what moves bring the best feeling to her. That saves time you falsely claim you don't have.

You have 168 hours for your weekly obligations. If you can't spend two hours on sex—the greatest, most pleasurable thing in the world—twice a week, you are messed up. Worse, even if statistics had not said it, sex twice a week is below average. And if you have it twice a month, you are only spending two hours on sex out of 720 hours you have in a month. You are giving just about nothing to sex, yet you take away foreplay and rush to penetration because you have no time. Isn't that sick? I believe your love life is ill. Even if you could hit it every day, not having one hour sacred for sex is inexcusable. I'm talking about one hour, but you can have a great sex—without skipping foreplay—in considerably less time. Sex is the most powerful human emotion. Don't take away anything that belongs to it. On the contrary, bring more to it. Savor that foreplay kiss until it's dry!

A romantic kiss increases sexual desire, as saliva contains a sex hormone that plays a role in sexual arousal. The longer and more passionately you kiss, the more testosterone gets released. Therefore, don't rush to insert a finger inside her when you're kissing. If you can't resist, keep it still. Fingers are not the main characters here. They play the supporting role. Their time to shine is later.

Once the heat intensifies, take her to bed without losing lip connection. As she lies there, give her the appropriate kisses—unique to you two. Move with kisses from her cheek, chin, neck, shoulders, nipples (a bit of sucking wouldn't hurt) to your heading downtown. Once in downtown, your tongue should start a new journey that is long enough—and by "long enough," I mean as long as it takes—and then pass the torch to your fingers and penis.

The kissing started it; the kissing will end it. Give lots of it, even if she's just crashed after she or both of you came. She might not feel the whipped cream on top of the cake, but you have made the cake particularly beautiful. This is one of the special ways to seal a sexual adventure. What's a job well done if you neglect a small detail?

Use the following recommendations for all sexual kisses, and add your particularity.

❑ The Recommended To-Do List

- Make sure your lips aren't dry or cracked.
- Keep lip balm on hand.
- Rely on a breath mint or gum to keep your mouth fresh. At home, it's a good idea to brush your teeth and rinse your mouth with mint mouthwash right before the action.

❑ The Recommended Not-to-Do List

- Shove your entire tongue into his or her mouth.
- Let the saliva build-up become a flood. (Take a two-second break to swallow it.)
- Bite lips hard.

- Go full speed into a heavy make-out session.
- Prolong a single kiss.
- Be afraid to use your body language to tell your lover what you like and don't like.
- Continue a session that's dead or end it abruptly.

❑ The Benefits of Sexual Kisses

- They increase self-esteem.
- They lower stress and cholesterol levels.
- They help lovers to bond.
- They reduce stress and anxiety.
- They boost the immune system.
- They strengthen facial muscles.
- Erotic kisses light the candles for the birthday party.

❑ The Kissing Supplement

In many instances, a kiss is followed by a hug. The origins of hugging seem to be unknown, but in one hypothesis, the word *hug* could be related to the old Scandinavian word *hugga*, which means "to comfort." The second hypothesis is that the word hug is related to the German word *hegen*, which means "to foster or cherish" and originally meant to enclose with a hedge.

Depending on culture, context, and relationship, a hug demonstrates familiarity, brotherhood, friendship, flirting, love, affection, support and consolation, comfort, and sympathy in most countries and communities. A hug usually demonstrates affection and emotional warmth when we're reunited with someone after a long absence. A nonreciprocal hug demonstrates a relational problem.

Boxers traditionally hug each other after the final round to show peace and brotherhood and after the winner is announced to show congratulations. Young children hug their parents and siblings for love. In Portugal and Brazil, it is common among males to end letters, emails, and messages with the word *hug* or *hugs*.

Like kissing, hugging is a social behavior with health benefits. It increases levels of oxytocin and reduces blood pressure. Hugging a romantic partner before a stressful situation lessens the release of the stress hormone cortisol in women.

And then, there is cuddling, a related form of physical intimacy, where someone wraps his or her arms around a family member's, friend's, or lover's body. Cuddling is a more affectionate and intimate embrace, normally lasting a few minutes to hours. In contrast to hugging, cuddling is usually shared between two people who are lying down together in an intimate manner. Cuddling also causes the body to release oxytocin. The popularity of kissing and hugging is such that January 21 and July 6 are designated as international kissing and hugging days, respectively. And February 14 (Valentine's Day) is the international date for the celebration of love, with hugs and kisses and sex. Never lose an opportunity to wrap a kiss with a hug.

Erotic kissing is the best, as it causes a release of oxytocin, the "love hormone," which stirs up feelings of affection and attachment, and dopamine, the "reward hormone." It's the first step toward the doors of the greatness of life—relationship and sex. Whether kissing will land a great wife or husband in your lap is not important. The importance is that although erotic kissing is a small portion of life's pie, it is part of the most powerful human act—sex. That alone causes powerful emotions.

We kiss for love, luck, and pleasure or to say hello or goodbye. I feel sorry for the 10 percent who don't kiss, as well as those who should but don't. I hope we adjust our attitudes and give kissing the honor it deserves, particularly erotic kisses.

3

Masturbation

Many animals masturbate, both male and female, with and without partners. It has been observed in cats, dogs, rhinoceroses, monkeys, chimpanzees, bonobos, sheep, bharal or blue sheep, dwarf cavies, white-tailed deer, zebras, takhi horses, warthogs, and hyenas, to mention a few. In fact, evidence of stimulation of the genitals with objects is found in several primates and cetaceans. A variety of creative techniques are used, including front paws, feet, flippers, and tails. This is sometimes accompanied by stimulation of the nipples, observed in rhesus macaques and bonobos. Apes and monkeys use a variety of objects to masturbate and even deliberately implement sexual stimulation in creative ways. Birds masturbate by mounting tufts of grass, mounds of earth, and leaves. Some mammals, such as primates and dolphins, rub their genitals against the ground or other surfaces for direct or indirect stimulation of the clitoris. Inhibiting or punishing domestic animals for masturbation often leads to increased masturbation. Castration does not prevent masturbation.

Myths and misconceptions continue to spread ideas that masturbation is harmful, while masturbation has tons of benefits, such as boosting hormones and chemicals that promote positive emotions and feelings, as it triggers the release of hormones and chemicals in the brain's pleasure-reward center. It also releases hormones and neurotransmitters to help reduce stress and blood pressure, while promoting relaxation, which makes it easier to fall asleep.

A study of 778 adults found that good sleep is associated with orgasm. Masturbation reduced the time it took to fall asleep and improved sleep quality. The only concern is being heard or seen by others. Aside from that, you can explore what brings you satisfaction, to a strong orgasm, without bias or fear of sexually transmitted diseases. It's sad that not all women explore their treasure lands on solo adventures. (Yes, I said explore, and you should take note.)

Fortunately, there are four types of masturbation: self, given, received, and mutual. Any one is pleasurable and healthy. All should be on your sex menu, and frequently, they should be the special of the day.

Since there is not much to describe with male masturbation, let's focus on the female's solo fun.

Self-masturbation. Practice makes perfect, and solo exploration is the best way to discover what works for you and why. Some women attest to having greater sexual confidence with their partners and to enjoying sex more than those who avoid masturbation.

Mutual masturbation. Still pleasurable, mutual masturbation is a low-grader, a multitask. The attention is split between enjoyment of what you're receiving and your obligation to give. For that, the principle of sixty-nine applies here: as the arousal intensifies, the partner approaching orgasm is the one to be a receiver only. Never focus on coming both at same time, and don't rush yourself to come either. Just go with the flow.

Given masturbation. This one is about 70 percent pleasure for the receiver and 30 percent for the giver. It's a great way to show appreciation to your partner and give a boost to the relationship. You should give it to your man much more often. The biological construct allows men to enjoy masturbation more often than women, but it's shorter. That doesn't mean that men shouldn't surprise women with masturbation every now and then. When you do, don't be sneaky—keep a masturbation session at just that, unless she wants more.

Receiving masturbation. You lie there and let someone stimulate your genitals until the end of it. (I say "until the end of it" because every time we start a sexual act, we are thinking orgasm, and that does not happen every time.) For pleasure enhancement, use your tongue, mouth, hands, and fingers to caress and nibble her breasts and other erogenous zones.

It's a misconception that sexually active people, especially those in committed relationships, don't need to masturbate. That's not true. We simply allow other sexual activities to push masturbation away. Only sexual dysfunction should take it away. And if so, it's recommended that you fix the problem. During this search and practice of what brings you the ultimate pleasure, turn every stone, and mark the most important ones. A friend of mine once said, "A good masturbation is better than any sex." I don't entirely agree with that, but I understand his point.

A wife never had seen a man pleasuring himself, so she asked her husband to masturbate for her. Halfway there, she had to be penetrated. She later told him, "Seeing you stroking your dick, turning your head side to side, your facial expression, and all your body movements made me so horny I couldn't resist to fuck." This attests that watching someone masturbate is extremely arousing—to the point of no return.

Whether or not to masturbate is a personal choice. I lament if you choose not to, and hope you've found ways to compensate for the loss.

4

Tragedy of Ignorance vs. Power of Knowledge

☿

> I was at the farm, close to home. I felt something strange inside my vagina. And it kept on increasing. I checked myself and saw blood soaking my underwear. I stopped ever thing I was doing [and] ran home crying. My mom heard me.
>
> She came out in panic, too. "Marianne, why are you crying? What happened?"
>
> I shouted, "Mama, I'm dying!"
>
> When I showed her how badly I was bleeding, she said, "You are not dying. You're a woman now, Marianne."
>
> And she taught me a little about menstrual cycles and how to avoid pregnancy.

A teenager living under a strict mom's rules, where hanging out with friends and dating were not allowed, promised her mom that she would sleep with everybody when she got her freedom. She became a mother at nineteen. Unfortunately, her sexual journey wasn't pretty. At age thirty-three, she had more kids than she could handle. The doctors tied her tubes to save her life.

Thousands of families, including innumerable teen moms, live in poverty, misery, and disappointment, with low odds for success due to sexual ignorance. The blame goes to all who have stood in the way of sexual education.

A father came home to hear his fifteen-year-old saying "I love you" on the phone. This was how he found out that she had a boyfriend. He took her phone away instead of educating her about relationships and sex.

In such an open world nowadays, teenagers know a lot about sex, but they don't necessarily have the right knowledge. Parents should give greater attention to the sexual education of their children. Sadly, numerous parents make the mistake of punishing instead of educating.

Here's a male friend's story:

> On a hot and humid Tuesday afternoon, my neighbor and I were at the farm. The relentless heat forced us to seek relief in the shade. We talked for a while about random subjects including relationships. We asked each other how many kids we wished to have, where to live, when to get

married, and so on, and then we started flirting. She gave me clue after clue that she wanted to do something, but nothing happened because I didn't know what to do. I should've told my friends about it and probably be prepared for the next time, but I didn't. I was afraid of them telling on me.

My second chance was at eighteen, about six months after I started working at a government-owned enterprise. A hot, slender, and enthusiastic girl was very much in love with me. I didn't react right away to her moves because she wasn't my type—she was a mother—but my friends convinced me to go out with her for the fun of it, which I did! We went for a walk after work and ended up at the high school grounds. After a long conversation about her past boyfriend, she kissed me, and we started making out. I needed an easy pass that didn't come. She resisted some of my moves, and that made it awkward for me. I guess standing-up sex is what she wanted. I tried my best to do a good job, but it was in vain. My inexperience and poor sexual knowledge and understanding of female anatomy added to my discomfort and lack of confidence. I couldn't get it in or even close to her vagina.

I am still mad about that adventure, and honestly, I don't understand why she didn't use her experience instead of counting on my sexual abilities, which I am sure she realized, soon we started making out, that I didn't have. I knew a lot in my head, but my big problem was that I didn't know how to take charge, be confident, and all that. I was stupid. Anyway, three years later, I had sex for the first time. I knew what to do and how. It was comfy, with confidence. Not a celebration or extraordinary event but a job well done. I was happy with it.

I have no doubt there are tons of stories similar to this one throughout the entire world, and many more will happen. I just hope that none is yours. Whether you're a virgin or have put a million miles on your sexual wagon, never stop learning about human behavior, sexuality, and the power of sex. Ignorance is a predicament, and knowledge is eternal power.

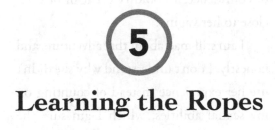

5

Learning the Ropes

In my day, culture, myths, and taboos demanded protection for girls as the way to save their virginity for marriage, recommended relationships after graduation, and endorsed sexual pleasure after marriage. I credit this philosophy for higher school graduation rates and low teenage pregnancy, but the consequences outweigh the benefits.

Sex is one of the most powerful acts that controls every aspect of our well-being and success. If we are sex-illiterate and we don't have it on a regular basis, our lives are a flight doomed to failure. Unless you're asexual, this statement sure sounds dramatic—until you realize the power of sex. Sex is what drives us to seek social bonds and relationships. An individual who is antisocial, single, and doesn't care about sex is on low level of human greatness. Sexual dissatisfaction is the number-one reason for separation or divorce, and poor sex is driven by sexual ignorance. Being sexually ignorant is like canoeing on the pond to kill frustration instead of cruising the world to discover and enjoy the wonders of sex and relationships.

Innumerable youngsters who became teen moms and fell into the cracks and abyss of welfare, as well as countless abortions that resulted in death, are examples of tragedies perpetrated by sexual ignorance. Religions, churches, and other entities that aim to control society know those facts, yet they abide by myths, taboos, and misconceptions to guard sex with fence and barbed wire, soldiers, and vicious dogs. (Unbelievable!) This makes learning the ropes much harder, yet it's an obligation you must fulfill.

It doesn't matter how sexually illiterate we are; we will enjoy sex. Instinct is sufficient for sexual pleasure, but that's just getting a passing grade. To achieve an honorable-student diploma, you must be an ace by using critical thinking to find all the t's to cross and i's to dot. Unfortunately, this process is hard. The crazy physical and biological changes you face in adolescence put you in an I-don't-give-a-shit mood, making it easy to neglect your sexual education. Try your best and use determination as your best tool, as well as great teachers and supportive friends. Don't walk blindfolded. Your parents are your sight, and they will be more willing to educate you when you ask for it. Ask them throughout your life. Aside from them, there are many ways to get sexual education, such as from friends, school counselors, sex therapists, sexologist, doctors, and online articles. Since sex is the most powerful human act, the more you know, the more you need to know.

❑ The Time to Start

The time to start having sex depends on many factors, such as personality, culture, tradition, religion, and philosophy, among other things, but most importantly, education. Considering that the main purpose of sex is reproduction, we are ready, biologically, to start sex at puberty. Once a girl gets her first menstruation and a boy can ejaculate, they can procreate. But is nine to fourteen years of age the time to start having sex? Of course not. Maybe that was the right time millions of years ago. This is another mystery of humankind. I believe being ready to procreate in puberty is just preparation for motherhood and fatherhood, rather than the time to start having fun under the sheets.

Researchers found that two-thirds of sexually active girls wish they had waited longer before having sex, and of seniors in high school, more than 70 percent of girls regret the sexual experiences they have had.

The early arrival of puberty can produce sex drives when teens aren't fully capable of understanding the social and biological consequences of sexual activities. In fact, the younger the adolescents who have any type of sexual relations, including oral sex, the higher the chances of catching a sexually transmitted infection or disease. Therefore, if you happen to have a high sex drive, and you are sexually active, you must focus your attention on knowing as much as you can about sex to minimize the chances of lifetime regrets.

One of the main reasons to be knowledgeable and enjoy sex is that sex is phenomenal and extremely important in our lives. It relieves stress, frustration, and depression; stimulates the mind; and improves the immune system, among other health benefits. It is the only pleasurable way to stay true to the continuity of the family tree. Yet it carries many side effects, some of which can disturb your life up to death. Even though these effects don't discriminate, the younger you are, the greater the odds of being a prime target, as immaturity sells you out to the bad guys, which I call *the shadows of death*—sexually transmitted infection or disease (STI or STD) and unwanted pregnancy. These bad guys lurk under the bed to strike you hard after you've enjoyed a moment of pleasure without protection. For the most part, they sneak up on you with minor infections that you can get rid of in no time, almost hassle-free. But they can also grab you by the neck and slam you down with serious infection or an incurable disease.

Studies have concluded the following:

Each year, up to ten million American teenagers contract a sexually transmitted infection, with HPV (human papillomavirus), followed by trichomoniasis and chlamydia, as the most common STI diagnoses.

Genital herpes and gonorrhea combined account for about 12 percent. HIV, syphilis, and hepatitis B account for less than 1 percent, but young people accounted for about 20 percent of all new HIV diagnoses in the United States in 2011. In 2020, almost two-thirds (61 percent) of all reported chlamydia cases were among people fifteen to twenty-four years of age. That reflects a 15 percent decrease among fifteen-to-nineteen-year-olds, yet it is considered high.

Teenagers do not understand the risks associated with sexual activities. They think there are fewer risks associated with oral sex than intercourse, but oral sex can transmit chlamydia, genital herpes, gonorrhea, and syphilis. This poor knowledge drives teenage girls to give oral sex to many boys as if it was nothing, studies have concluded. They soon wake up with bitterness in their mouths, way before their first vaginal intercourse. (Once you become involved in sexual activities with more than one partner, your risk of getting an infection or disease increases in direct proportion to the number of partners.)

You may not care because none of your friends who are playing this dangerous game has ever had a sexual infection, and you feel knowledgeable on this subject. Well, you could be fooling yourself and seriously shoot yourself in the foot. The numbers don't lie. Since sexual shadows of death swim in the oceans and have strong currents to pass infections and diseases rapidly to other people—and some infections give no sign of their invasion of your privacy—it is your responsibility to educate and protect yourself.

To start having sex at a young age is a clear indication

of poor knowledge about sex, and that has consequences. There is no need to rush and run the risk of getting the whipping from bad sexual experiences. Common sense says if you're not sure and you don't know enough about sex, it's not the time for you to start.

❑ The Umbrellas

Considering the frequency and danger of this game, we need umbrellas to protect us from the dust, wind, sun, rain, and snow. Protection is our umbrella; it is a bodyguard that is lightning fast and is powerful, like Hulk. Any time we have sex without protection, it's only luck that saves us from the beatings of STI/STD and unwanted pregnancy.

Some sex educators and Christian organizations advocate abstinence as the most important chapter of sex education, and they recommend sexual abstinence until marriage. When it comes to protection, nothing beats abstinence. The problem is that anyone who would have sex but abstains is missing the greatest ingredient of life. "She needs to get laid" is a comment we hear all the time about a woman known to be single and crazy. A physician asks patients about their sex lives and recommends sexual intercourse on a regular basis for health reasons.

In the late 1960s to early '70s, our church demanded that women wear skirts no shorter than a couple of inches above the knees and that wives wear nothing that showed any skin above the knees. Those who refused would be temporarily banned from church, could not take Communion, and were not allowed to have their children baptized. The worst offenders would be banned from church activities forever. The purpose was to curb sexual desires, which then would reduce the chances of having sex before marriage. So many single women chose the punishment rather than lengthening their skirts. Abstinence, despite being an ace in this game, didn't go far at the start of the sexual revolution, and it doesn't now. But there are many other powerful cards to serve as an umbrella for STI/STD. Pick the ones that are easily workable for you and that go with your morality and philosophy.

❑ **The Numbers**

Different countries and cultures honor a different number of partners for average experience before a committed relationship. Research and surveys show that having sex with many partners before marriage is better than with just a couple. In recent years, women who had ten or more partners have been the most likely to divorce. This gives us three to nine partners, on average, before marriage. The problem is that about 10 percent of men and 6 percent of women have admitted to increasing or decreasing the numbers, depending on the circumstances. This happens because antiquated social expectations lead men to believe they need to give impressive numbers, and women feel the need to decrease their numbers so they aren't judged as promiscuous. Women who had had sex with one partner or were virgins before marriage (this is a fast-shrinking population) were the least likely to divorce.

Well, there's no such thing as an average or magic number to grant happy relationships or great sex. There are simply numbers and, more importantly, the application of knowledge acquired by numbers. Sexuality is not a product you can buy or trophies you collect. Sexuality is the gift we all receive, distinct for each of us. The number of sexual partners doesn't define your worthiness; the strength of your character (education, love and care, personal development, among other traits) does. Maybe it's true that guys are more fascinated with numbers than girls, since they brag more, but it's not because they are dogs or are the sole product of their sexual greediness. Rather, it is an impulsive desire ingrained in their DNA for sexual intercourse with many partners to increase the chances of procreation and finding the best mate. This applies to women, too. So, women could and should be as fascinated as men with numbers. I am sure that all who aren't fascinated with numbers are as human as all who are, and they may be enjoying the sex more.

The ropes of sexuality are tricky and can extend from here to Cape Verde (my country) and back, and each section is tricky. It's very important that you give equal attention to all sections of learning the ropes. Learn them well, decide which ones serve best, and then proceed to master them and continue to learn.

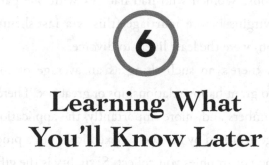

6

Learning What You'll Know Later

When we were young and full of joy, energy, and enthusiasm, we saw no obstacles to success. We saw old people struggling and suffering, but that was them. Suddenly, adulthood knocked on the door. Soon after, midlife hit us. We were not happy. We went through changes and obstacles we didn't see coming, and the joys and surprises we dreamed of never came. If we'd only known! Well, lucky you, reading this chapter! Here, you will learn some aspects of life that you can control and some that you can't. All, individually or collectively, will affect your sexuality to the end.

We are insufficiently developed to think about the future in our prime years. If we do, we see more fantasy than reality. After age fifty (earlier for some, later for others), a lot of what we had taken for granted starts to limp. There lies the ugliness of life—poverty and financial trouble (the main culprits for most of our stress and frustration); sexually transmitted diseases and infections; inherited diseases, mental disorders, and physical impairment; sleep deprivation; drugs and alcohol abuse; diabetes and cardiovascular diseases (such as high blood pressure and high cholesterol); libido decline and erectile dysfunction; as well as many other things of life's phenomena that are detrimental to our success, relationships, and sexual enjoyment. The future looks dark, depressing, and frightening. It's better that we leave it alone—except we have no choice but to face it.

Don't let your youth fool you that whatever comes your way will be crushed! The fun and feelings of invulnerability that we experience now are not forever. All who have said, "If I knew then what I know now" wore the shoes of life you're wearing now. Be wise; if you buy an umbrella before the rainstorm, you will win big! Lots of life's phenomena can throw us off the wagon. You might become someone who is impossible to be with; who is incapable of staying employed or being a successful businessperson; or who is socially, mentally, and physically unfit for daily activities. You might become addicted to drugs and alcohol, have an abusive spouse, or become a victim of barbaric acts of men or a tragic natural event. Any such ailments can hinder your sex life, and many of them can hit you. Under such circumstances, any sexual journey is severely attacked and left for dead. You must protect yourself from the start.

During youth, it's easy to not appreciate what you have. The smoothness of your girlfriend's skin, the fullness and shine of her hair, the scent of her body, the slenderness of her physique, and her kissable lips on her beautiful face escape the sight of your soul. Her mouth is so warm and delicious, her tongue is pleasurable, her breasts are firm and erect, and the vulva is pretty and amazing and engorges ferociously. Her pelvic muscles are strong. Her vagina is robust, with abundant lubrication, and she gets horny more often than she can afford. She has energy, enthusiasm, and eagerness to serve and be served, and she shows love and desire intensely. Every touch is pleasurable, every kiss is erotic, and every orgasm feels better. Sex with her is crazy fun, crazy pleasurable, and an amazing workout.

Sadly, instead of indulging with honor and distinction in her entire greatness, you simply like her a lot or love her a little. Having lots of sex is your priority. Also, because your strength and endurance are extraordinary, you're impressive. Any girl in your arms feels secure, warm, and happy. Your libido is insane—you're ready to hit it anywhere, anytime, all day, and all night with your frequent rock-hard erection. You just care about having fun.

Likewise, she will not appreciate you fully because she's surrounded by your peers. She's open for business, and the customers flow abundantly. That's youth, when we do things for fun. We are incapable of and not interested in realizing that we must enjoy fully what we have now because it won't last forever and that we should care for the future.

We are victims of the following: "Young, stupid, and full of cum is what we are! Leave us alone!" Please avoid this trap.

The common triggers of "If I'd known then what I know now" come from regrets that middle-aged and older people have over what they could've done but didn't. For example, there was a girl or boy who came our way, but we despised that person because they were ugly or not our type. We were not sure if a fresh friend was being just that or wanted us to make a move. Our best friend's lover wanted us, but we refused because we were honoring loyalty, only see them split shortly after, and our chances of partying vanished.

A woman told me she would never forget her greatest mistake. She had been deeply in love with her boyfriend. He suggested sex, but she told him to wait until marriage. A few months later, he died in a car accident. She couldn't forgive herself and lived with regrets. When people approach you with compliments for what you have (a boyfriend or girlfriend) and tell you to enjoy yourselves, they see in both of you what they lost due to inexperience, stupidity, and ignorance. Their hidden message is, "Love and appreciate each other. Make love to her. Treat her right, every chance you have, in the best way you can."

They are right! Therefore, kiss and appreciate her, head to toe. Be wise and creative. Turn every stone in her treasure land. And you, the sexy, beautiful princess, squeeze every drop of juice out of him. Be there for him as much as you can. Allow and demand that he gives you what you deserve. Suck him well, ride him hard, make him go crazy. If you lose each other, there won't be regrets or laments.

Don't wait until you can't get an erection without drugs, your joints hurt, you rely on alcohol and medication for survival, or your vagina cries out loud, even before anything gets close to her, to start chasing a young woman or man to close your sexual wounds. Rather, enjoy all you can now, when you are desirable and powerful. You need not live as if there's no tomorrow (unless you want to and suffer the consequence tomorrow. And that's a bad idea). Just be wise to enjoy today, encompassing all the treasures of your lover.

To learn what you will know later is to put yourself ahead of the game so that you probably never will say, "If I'd known then what I know now."

Erogenous Zones

What are the areas on the body that are sensitive to stimulation, cause erotic feelings when touched, and generate erotic thought when visible? Both men and women have them, and women are the winners, day and night, in rain or shine. These areas take sex to intensely pleasurable levels, including orgasms and multiple orgasms. Even less-important areas cause orgasms to about 12 percent of women. What are these areas? The erogenous zones—and here they are:

❏ **Men's**

- Lips and tongue
- Neck
- Breasts and nipples
- Glans (the penis head)
- Frenulum
- Testicles
- Perineum
- Prostate

- Anus
- Scrotum
- Inner thighs
- Anus

❏ **Women's**

- Scalp
- Earlobes
- Lips and tongue
- Neck
- Areolas and nipples
- Armpits, inner arms, and arms
- Hands and fingers
- Naval and lower stomach
- Lower back
- Pubic mound
- Commissure
- Clitoris
- Vagina (entrance, G-spot, A-spot)
- Cervix
- Frenulum
- Perineum
- Butt cheeks
- Anus
- Inner thigh
- Behind the knee

- Ankles
- Bottom of feet and toes

The genitals, anus, breasts, and the mouth are primary erogenous zones, but it's hard not to think of his crotch or her "down there," let alone a woman's third most erogenous zone—breasts. We forget breasts are much more than a great contribution to her beauty, attraction, nourishment for newborns, and nutrition for men's eroticism. Breasts, especially the nipples, are fundamental sexual players.

Scientists believe sexual attraction to breasts is the result of their function as a secondary sex characteristic. And the world has so much to say about them. Many cultures, for example, regard bare breasts in public as immoral or indecent, while others allow upper-body nudity on beaches, even full-body nudity. The US culture prefers breasts to be youthful and upright, while other cultures venerate women with drooping breasts. Many women regard their breasts as a symbol of sexual attractiveness, a sign of femininity, and important to self-esteem. Some women with beautiful breasts don't feel superior, and others with small breast do not feel less feminine. Some women with small breasts feel less attractive, while women with big, firm breasts enjoy showing off their cleavage and feel sexually empowered. I am pretty sure these women know that modern female fashions that focus on clothing that facilitate display of cleavage is attributed to an increase in breast fetishism. Display of cleavage is also regarded as a form of female flirting and seduction and is erotic. Heterosexual men get erotic thoughts from seeing a woman's breasts and get aroused by touching them. You might be surprised to know that staring at women's breasts cuts the risk of heart attack and stroke in half (improves blood circulation, lowers blood pressure) and extends a man's life by four or five years. Scientists recommend that men over forty years old look at full-breasted women for more than ten minutes daily to achieve the best results.

Like the vulva, the characteristics, shape, and color of breasts varies from woman to woman. No two breasts are identical, and no two women have the same breasts. The response to stimulation also varies. Therefore, be proud of your construct, and get the best out of what you've got. It bothers me that we don't explore breasts more during a sexual adventure. By the way, treat both breasts by the rules of democracy—equal pleasure. The great pair of erogenous zones give orgasms to numerous women.

Because of sexuality traits, erogenous zones are not one-size-fits-all. Some women are driven to ecstasy by caresses on their lower backs or tongue-sweeps across their toes, while the same actions are nothing more than an annoying tickle to others. Therefore, ask your lover about her secondary erogenous zone, and don't be surprised if the answer is, "I don't really know." In this case, you can touch them to discover the hidden spots. Experts recommend a sex feather to be more effective.

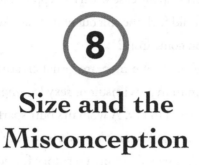

Size and the Misconception

It can be complicated to explain the reasons for the fascination and misconceptions of size, as reality, fantasy, individual preference, culture, and tradition turn them into a dilemma. I believe that a detailed look into this matter will help to lift the fog, and then we can see beyond what's been given to us (sometimes forced) to believe and worship.

❑ Big Butt

As I stepped inside the building, there she was again—this beautiful, sexy girl in her early thirties, wearing tight silk pants, with her underwear lines easily visible and her buttocks irresistible to a man's eyes. For a short moment, my imagination went wild, and a rush of blood flooded my crotch. I know size means nothing, but my mind was in denial. I tried to dull my mind and blur my vision, but I couldn't resist looking at her one more time before I entered the cafeteria. Shortly after, a man in his sixties didn't help my case when he stepped into the cafeteria and said, "I would fuck the shit out of that ass." Where does all this fascination come from?

Biological traits. We men are visual creatures. We see a beautiful woman in a swimsuit or sexy leggings, and we are instantly attracted to her. A woman's butt sparks our sexual fantasy and staring. We aren't perverts; we are what we are!

Anal sex is a sexual act on a territory forbidden to enter without permission. Forbiddance awakens curiosity—since we can't have it, we want it even more. This explains the popular saying that sex with a best friend, a mistress, or in public has an extra element—an increase of pleasure because of forbiddance. This is also the reason we guys are obsessed with sex positions that facilitate rear entry. We feel like we're breaking the rules to gain access to a danger zone. Therefore, it seems that, instinctively, we stare at women's butts because they might not see us doing it. And "bigger" is more eye-catching. And there's more!

Evolutionary psychologists suggest that we are attracted to big butts because they are a visual indication of the woman's youth and fertility. One study found that men subconsciously prefer women with a spinal curvature on a forty-five-degree angle. "This spinal structure would have enabled pregnant women to balance their weight over the hips," enabling these women to be more effective at seeking nutrition "during pregnancy and less likely to suffer spinal injuries"; therefore, being a partner "better able to provide for fetus and offspring, and … carry out multiple pregnancies … without injury." Omega-3 fatty acids, which are crucial for the baby's brain development, are in the mother's breast milk and in butt and thigh fats. Big butts are venerated in many cultures and communities by women and men.

Discipline and self-care. A big butt signifies she's working out and eating right to maintain her highly desired gift. Pictures and video posts online (especially Instagram and Snapchat) taken during workouts attest to that.

Pillows. Many guys admitted that butts are like pillows. They have a place to rest their heads and fall asleep peacefully. It is heaven for them.

Emotional intelligence. Some scientists believe girls develop emotional intelligence around the time they gain curves—in puberty—and that girls with big butts understand more quickly and are more intuitive than girls with flat butts.

Like drugs. A study proved that big butts affect the same region in men's brains that is triggered by alcohol and drugs.

Health benefits. Girls who have big butts are not in danger of getting sick from a chronic illness, as the extra fat in the butt is harmless in comparison with fat in other regions of the body, which can cause coronary disease.

Environment. Big butts are extremely popular in today's culture. Women are seen as sex symbols and are very desirable. Such reality is pushed ferociously by the media and hip-hop music, where Nicki Minaj is considered the leader, especially on the song "Anaconda."

Attractive. Fuller butts enhance the appearance of the curvature of the spine, giving the hourglass figure and making the woman look very attractive.

Treasure exhibition. Some men dating, engaged to, or married to a sexy woman with a big butt feel blessed and are proud to show off. Big butts also increase a man's relationship satisfaction and pride.

Anchor in bed. A big butt gives her an edge in bed. A friend of mine is fascinated with big butts, if they aren't fake. For him, they look amazing and increase his arousal during sex, especially doggy, because he likes "watching the bouncing of her big, fat ass when I am fucking them hard."

I believe all guys are suckers for the hourglass figure. Most guys like women with big butts, yet supermodels almost never have big butts.

❑ Big Penis

A friend of mine was surprised to know how popular it's been for men to exchange pictures and videos of their bodies with women. Two weeks later, he showed me a reply text from a woman ("Oh, wow! Let me fly home for a feast") after she saw a picture of his penis.

Back home, a mentally ill youth had a reputation for carrying big material. A woman who heard the news tried it out and continued her forbidden satisfaction for years. After Joanna Doe experienced a one nightstand, she went insane after being ghosted. She eventually got hold of him by phone. "I want you to fuck me one more time. Just one" she said. She gave him anything he wanted. It wouldn't surprise me if almost all women would like to try it. A big penis is often the main topic when women talk about sex.

Many individuals have below-average as well as above-average sizes. Plenty of small penises are considered gifted among certain people, and big penis are considered small among certain people. Contrary to popular opinion, statistics show that blacks aren't the king; Latinos are.

The ten countries with the smallest erect penis length in inches are as follows:

1. Cambodia—3.95 inches
2. Taiwan—4.24
3. Philippines—4.27
4. Sri Lanka—4.29
5. Hong Kong—4.41
6. Bangladesh—4.41
7. Thailand—4.51
8. Vietnam—4.52
9. Malaysia—4.52
10. Singapore—4.54

The ten countries with the largest erect penis length in inches are as follows:

1. Ecuador—6.93 inches
2. Cameroon—6.56

3. Bolivia—6.50
4. Sudan—6.48
5. Haiti—6.30
6. Senegal—6.26
7. Gambia—6.25
8. Netherlands—6.25
9. Cuba—6.25
10. Zambia—6.21 inches

The popular twelve inches that society claims belongs to black men can't be found anywhere, but various online sites show that after the death of Roberto Esquivel Cabrera in February 2022, the man with the world's largest penis (18.9 inches), Brooklyn native Jonah Falcon, 52, took first place with a measurement of 13.5 inches long and 8 inches girth when erect.

The online comments about him vary from insults of his looks and hygiene, to sympathy for his troubles, to sarcasm—such as that he needs suspenders on his underwear; that he belongs in a horse stable; and that Shaquille O'Neal doesn't believe the story. There wasn't much praise for his huge size or any admiration or jealousy, except a suggestion for him to make a living on pornography. Some interesting comments said that guys who are too big have a hard time finding long-term relationships; that this man has to find a woman who is deep and wide; more isn't necessarily better; anything bigger than eight inches is a liability; it's not what you've got, it's what you do with it and how you use it; and a satisfaction with the average seven to nine inches from a woman who left a relationship with a man who was big because it was not only uncomfortable and painful but also a "complete waste of time. Apparently, he thought his size automatically made it good, desirable … he couldn't have been more wrong. Size does not matter."

Surveys say the majority of woman prefer a big penis for a one-night stand or a short-term relationship and a little bigger than average size for a long-term relationship.

❑ Big Breasts

A standing theory holds that breasts evolved with a secondary purpose, which is signaling to men a woman's sexual maturity, fertility, and nutritional advantage, thus making her a promising mate. Large breasts have higher levels of the hormone estradiol, simply defined as a sex hormone, that's necessary for maintaining sexual and reproductive health; it's produced mainly by the ovaries.

Large breasts come with inconveniences, such as the following:

- Back pain
- Need of a bra
- Difficulties finding clothing that fits comfortably
- Discomfort when playing sports
- Annoyance of men staring and making "boob jokes"

- Sleep discomfort
- Difficulty when breastfeeding (Newborns push their faces against the breast to suck on the nipple.)

In the meantime, the following benefits far outweigh the consequences:

- Beauty. Breasts enhance the beauty of a woman.
- Attention/Attraction. Men can't resist the pull toward a woman with big breasts, and they are more willingly to help her in any possible way. (My heart beats faster when I am close to big breasts and instantly want her to be mine.)
- Cover. Big breasts not only enhance a woman's beauty but also cover her flaws. She could be less attractive physically and not beautified by clothes and makeup, but she draws attention with flirting when she has a pair of big breasts.
- Better gene quality.
- Preference. Women with big breasts are more likely to have an easy job interview and be hired quicker than women with small breasts. In fact, experts recommend women with small breasts use fillers to make the breasts look big for a job interview. Big breasts take the jackpot home for a night of fun ahead of small-breasted women.
- Eroticism. For men, large breasts are very attractive. Large-breasted women are more sensual. Sexually, they

are gentler and more relaxed in bed. They can give and receive more pleasure by erotic breast massage, one of the most popular secret fantasies of men and women. Touching the breasts during sex increases arousal and is incredibly pleasurable for men.

- Sex. Only big breasts allow for mammary intercourse.
- Convenience. Big breasts serve as a stand for cell phones, tablets, iPads, and laptop computers. (I found that interesting.)

❑ Big Lips

Both the top and bottom lips have their share of size fascination. Their best contribution goes to enhancement of a woman's beauty and sexual attraction. A nice set of kissable lips on a beautiful face seals the deal. They become irresistible to men's attention. They make a kissing session more erotic. According to clichés, when the upper lip is smaller than the bottom, the woman has nailed it by the Creator.

As to the bottom lips, women with fat labia look sexually hotter and more desirable and more confidence. They allow for more sexual play and may get more spontaneous arousal.

❑ The Intruders

For all that's trash and treasure, the media is the most powerful social driving force, able to turn lies and foggy phenomena into what will bring desirable results to the media itself and its engine. Its algorithm is too complex to digest, and its field of action is too broad to tackle. Family values and sexualization—especially teen sexualization—are deeply influenced by media, with the discovery that "sex sells." And pornography grabs the torches from media and takes them to new levels of distortion. "A man's got do what a man's got to do"— so do the enterprises.

Society has blamed the media for making up and perpetuating phrases such as the following:

- Black women are always angry and freaky in bed.
- Blondes are dumb.
- White people can't dance.
- Native Americans love to gamble.
- All Asians are geniuses
- Black people can't learn.

Your responsibility is to educate yourself and read between the lines.

Every race, community, culture, and ethnicity has a bigger- or smaller-than-average size. Only a small percentage of men is under the standard. There is no public study showing that Asian men are inferior human beings. On the contrary, black men—wrongly labeled kings of penis (third leg)—had been considered subhuman.

❏ Where Do Myths and Misconception Come From?

The main character here is sexual racism. Public records show that after the abolition of slavery in 1865, white Americans showed an increasing fear of racial mixture. The racial divide became strong as the concept of whiteness developed. There was a widely held belief that the uncontrollable lust attributed to blacks threatened the purity of the nation. This increased white anxiety about interracial sex gave birth to the Ku Klux Klan in 1867, which led to violence and terrorism against the black population. There was a rise in lynch-mob violence, as many black men were falsely accused of rape in an attempt to preserve whiteness and prevent a racial mix. Some racists wanted racial separation as prevention against interracial sexual activity. Mixed-race couples who chose to live together were sought out and lynched. The infamous case of Emmett Louis Till, who was lynched in 1955 at the age of fourteen, under the pretext that (according to public information) he was whistling at a white woman, when he was actually whistling for his own purposes, is a disturbing example.

Black men were depicted as being as violent owners of big penises and highly prone to behavior that was violent and inhumane. They were considered terrifying predators who targeted helpless victims, especially white women, and thus were capable of hurting white women in bed. Black women were stereotyped as Jezebels, which claimed black women often initiated sex outside of marriage and were generally sexually promiscuous. This misconception arose "from the first encounters between European men and African women." Truth is, as the men were not used to the extremely hot climate, they misinterpreted the women's poor clothing for vulgarity and that white men were having sex with black women because they were more lustful. In turn, black men would lust after white women in the same way.

Simply put, the misconception is that white men have sex with black women because they are freaks in bed, but white men don't want to marry black women because they are vulgar. Black men have sex with white women because they are freaks in bed, give blow jobs, and like black men's huge penises. Black men don't want to marry them because they don't cook. That's pretty much a big pile of trash dumped on society that's good for the purpose of racism.

Fortunately, studies show that from 1958 to 2007, US citizens who agreed with interracial marriage rose from less than 5 percent in 1958 to 95 percent in 2007, and the disapproval during the same period declined from 78 percent to 18 percent, roughly.

For what's worth it, misconceptions are immortal. If you're a white woman married to a black man, be ready for the question, "Is it true what they say about blacks?"

Many white men believe they don't measure up, while some blacks are discredited. A white friend encouraged me to push a friendship with a white woman who flirted with me a few times during casual conversation. I suggested the same to him, to which he replied, "I don't have a 'third leg.'" In different instances, two white women said, "Let me get the ruler," during flirting conversations with a black man. I've heard that a black man got this remark: "Sex was good, but you are not really black." Clearly, he was short of expectations, rooted in misconception. "I am black from the waist down" is a common saying among funny white guys when entertaining black friends.

❏ The Credit

We can't take all the credit away from sizes. First, we've concluded that size fascination is biological. A toddler may walk into the bathroom and say to his father, "Daddy, your pee-pee is big," even if it's small. Boys and girls talk about sizes during their preteens and throughout adulthood. When a friend looks at your naked body and utters, "Girl, you should be in pornography," she's complimenting your size. The credits are as follows:

o   Butt: round and firm, forming a forty-five-degree angle with the waist, which enhances men's sexual thoughts and arousal.

o   Penis: a little bigger than the average size, with a large head; short and thick instead of long and thin; much easier to get the woman off. The visual is very arousing when first exposed. Only a long penis will easily reach the A-spot and cervix, the two areas claimed to be pleasurable by sexual stimulation, and it makes a man look more handsome.

o   Breasts: firm; C or D cups stand out and are a great contribution to her physical attraction and men's erotic thoughts.

o   Vulva: fat, especially the lips, with a landing-strip look; increases a women's erotic look.

In the face of all this, should you or should you not get from humans what God didn't give you? Well, that's freedom of choice! Also, it's not all the time that God overrides human actions and desires or cares about the consequences. We have seen and heard about the glory as well as the tragic consequences of plastic surgery. Butt lifts and implants have taken the place of breast implants and augmentation. The choice is yours. Remember that no one carries a full, perfect package, or it's fake. Not everyone likes fake.

Every man wants a loving, caring, understanding, and educated woman. These qualities are not products of the size of her boobs, vulva, lips, or ass. Every woman wants a rich man, strong, determined, visionary, and family-oriented. These merits aren't measured by the size of his penis, biceps, chest, or ass. In fact, there are plenty of full-size men and women (real and fake) longing for a relationship, sex, and living. Have you forgotten that great things may come in small packages? Don't! And don't worry about your low score; rather, focus on your high performance.

A great sex session has nothing to do with the size of a penis or her butt and breasts. Sexual knowledge, paired with preference, love, care, and perseverance, is the name of the game. The brain is the commander in chief. Once it allows us to feel horny, we're halfway there. Once we apply the rules of the game—foreplay and a thorough exploration of the vulva before a variety of penetrations—any sexual session played right is a roller coaster thrill that ends with satisfaction, orgasm, and multiple orgasms. Are you a fool? Don't let myth, ignorance, and misconception choose for you. God created different sizes and shapes to fit different needs, wishes, and desires. Find what suits you. Remind yourself that nothing lasts forever, and everything requires maintenance.

Unfortunately, myth and misconception or popular unfounded science are the same as lies and rumors—when they stick around for so long, they become hard or impossible to dismiss. Don't lose sleep over size. It is biology and mysterious!

In summary, size matters—and matters not.

9

Vagina and Her Neighbors

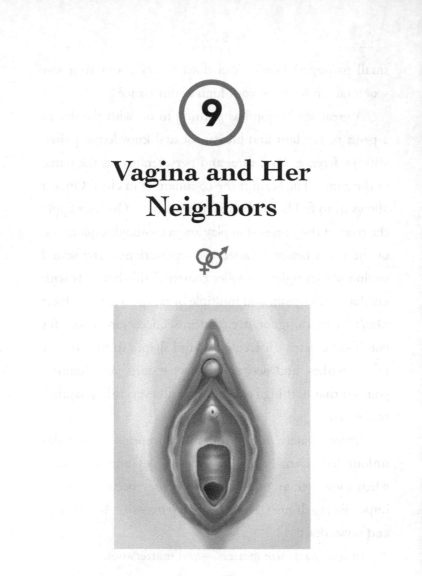

It is a blessing of the infinite intelligence that we humans communicate without much misunderstanding, despite using incomplete and confusing sentences, ambiguous and wrong words, distorted and incomplete descriptions, and poor interpretation of signs and body language during our daily interaction with society, families, and lovers. We are also inadequate in sexual communication.

Here's a joke, and I am putting it in mild terms: As the sexual penetration got heated, the woman uttered "I'm gonna pee. I'm gonna pee." And the man said, "Do something else, then, because I blocked the pee hole." Sure, this is a joke, but it is widely believed, especially among men, that women urinate through the vagina. It's a popular misconception that the sexual value of a woman is proportional to the quality and care of her vagina. Nothing is further from the truth, nor is the testimony that men lack knowledge of female anatomy or body-parts intricacy and functionality, especially when it comes to the vulva. Let's get educated, shall we?

Vulva. The "down there" we call the vagina is the vulva, a small, extremely amazing, and powerful treasure land, created to generate a sea of extraordinary pleasure. Sometimes we say vagina, but we mean vulva. Other times we mean vagina and labia—vaginal lips. Labia are components of the vulva. The labia are around the vagina and protect it. We say "fat vagina," but we mean fat labia. When she says, "I shaved my thing," she meant her mons pubis. Society promulgated a misleading description, and it never went away.

We are creatures that use sight as the main source of information about our surroundings. We gather sights, and the information goes to the brain for processing and the release of action, if necessary. That makes us vulnerable to the tricks of sight, brain, and mind. When we look at the "down there" of a naked female, we see the mounds first, then the labia, then the vaginal entrance, in order of mass. We look at the vaginal entrance because we are programmed to be familiar with it for its importance—intercourse. That made us give the vagina the Most Valuable Player title in our minds, not for what we see (we only see the entrance) but for the wonders she has. This trick is reinforced by the popular cultural and social misconception that we accumulate as we grow older. I also think there is this confusion or misconception because *pussy, vagina,* or *down there* sounds erotic, and *vulva* sounds sickening.

Back in high school, while on our lunch break, we were sitting on the benches of the school yard, picking on freshmen, talking shit to one another, and pranking on girls. Out of the blue, Rafael said, "Look at that girl! Her vagina is so big that she feels ashamed." We all turned our heads immediately to look at Christina's crotch.

My friend, his sister, and friends were sitting at the beach when he saw a girl walking in the distance. He said to his sister, "Pass me my glasses. I think that girl over there has a fat material."

My imagination went wild when a cousin-in-law once told us in a family get-together, "Mine are so fat that people can think I have two fists between my legs." She meant that her labia are very fat.

To be fair, *vagina* is the loudest mouth in the crowd and not the best speaker. It's a thing instead of the thing "down there," giving a great contribution to sexual pleasure, among other functions it has. Even people who are knowledgeable in the female sexual anatomy use the word vagina when they meant vulva, and they refer to lips as if lips are the parts of vagina, instead of components of the vulva. The credit goes to making a sexual conversation more easily understandable. Everybody falls for this trap, and no one cares. I believe is good to know what a cat is, even if you don't call it cat.

The following are the visible components of vulva, the "down there":

- Mons pubis
- Front commissure
- Frenulum
- Labia majora
- Clitoral hood
- Labia minora
- Clitoral glans
- Urethra
- Vaginal opening
- Vestibule
- Fourchette
- Perineum
- Anus

Let's describe each of them, but first, I did not come

across any conclusive results during my research for this book that state that pubic hair is one of the elements of the vulva. I found out that pubic hair roots lie in the sensorial zone and that some women get turned on when their pubic hair is teased out. That explains why my girlfriend was dripping juice while I shaved her vulva decades ago. Pubic hair is, in my view, part of the external parts of the vulva.

Pubic hair. This bush could mean nothing to you, but to the microscopic creature, this place is humongous. It serves three critical functions:

1. It protects the vagina from bacteria, pathogens, and dust;
2. It traps scents—pheromones—that alert males that you're biologically and/or emotionally ready to procreate, thus leading them to your promised land.
3. It functions as a cushion during sex.

It's a sign of pubertal age, and it's part of the trio that distinguishes children from adults. Back home, boys are men only after they have "three hairs"—beard, armpit hair, and pubic hair.

Many men like a bushy "down there," but shaved is a plus for most men (me included). Therefore, despite the importance of pubic hair, women have been motivated by pornography, female sexual expression and exploration, and other means to shave their pubic hair. Some women do shave occasionally to fulfill the wishes of their partners, and other shave for their own comfort. The bottom line is, shaving it or not seems to be matter of choice.

The mons pubis. This thick band of fatty tissue is covered in pubic hair. It's the love mound, as it forms a soft mound over the pubic bone. The mons veneris, or mountain of Venice, named after the Roman goddess of love, serves as cushion during sexual penetration and entices sexual attraction throughout sebaceous glands that secrete pheromones.

Labia majora (big, outer lips). Its outer sides are rich with pubic hair, while insides are smooth, lined with oily and sweat glands. Under the skin of the outer lips lies a network of erectile tissue that engorges with blood during arousal. It's not as sensitive as labia minora (small, inner lips) or other parts of the clitoral network, such as the head and shaft. Yet it's an important part of the treasure land.

Labia minora. They enfold around the clitoral head and wrap the entrance to the vagina. Like inside of the labia majora, inner lips are layered with oily glands that look and feel like tiny bumps. They vary in size and appearance from woman to woman, and no two lips of a woman may be the same. Some lips can have the combination of narrow, wide, curled inward or flared out, wrinkled and bumpy, smooth, and glossy, and others not so much so. During the process of arousal, they change color by engorgement.

The hood. As inner lips meet just above the clitoral head, they form protective hood, like the foreskin of a penis. When the clitoral hood rubs against the head, it produces powerful stimulation and pleasure. The hood also protects the head from overstimulation.

The front commissure, fourchette, and frenulum, all packed with nerve endings, play an important role in sexual arousal too. They bring pleasure when played with, and all respond to pressure and other forms of play.

Perineum. The small expanse of skin above the anus and beneath the vaginal entrance is the perineum. Beneath its skin lies a network of blood vessels and tissues that engorge during arousal and become highly sensitive to touch. Therefore, tactile stimulation of the area provides a great erotic arousal.

Anus. The anus is the opening where the gastrointestinal tract ends. It starts at bottom of the rectum, the last portion of the colon or large intestine, and is separated from the rectum by the anorectal line. The anus is approximately two to three inches long and packed with nerve endings—that's why it brings sexual pleasure, including orgasm.

Clitoris

Slightly above the urethra lies the most important female sexual organ, for which men lack knowledge, a phenomenal element of the vulva with the sole purpose of providing extensively great pleasure—the clitoris.

It is present in mammals, ostriches, and a limited number of other animals. In most species, the only function of the clitoris is to generate pleasure, but a few animals, including spotted hyenas, mate, urinate, and give birth through their large clitorises. In humans, its visible part—the glans, or head—is located just above the urethra opening at the junction of the inner lips. Like the penis, its size and sensitivity vary, but in general, the head is roughly the size and shape of a pea and has eight thousand to ten thousand nerve endings. Thus, the clitoris is the most sensitive erogenous zone and the primary source of sexual pleasure. The head retracts and disappears under its protective hood during peak arousal to avoid the pain of overstimulation, especially when the party gets hot and untamed or after an orgasm. Its size won't change as drastically as a penis when sexually stimulated, but there's a noticeable increase.

Although women who have given birth may have significantly larger clitorises, there is no correlation between the size of the clitoral head and a woman's age, height, weight, or use of hormonal contraception or being postmenopausal. The variation in clitoral size does not affect a woman's pleasure.

Debates have focused on the anatomical accuracy of the clitoris, the significance of its role in female sexual pleasure, its size and depth, and beliefs as to enlargement, mutilation, and piercing, but education of the clitoris is significantly hindered by cultural views, misconception, and prejudice. The understanding of its existence, anatomy, and importance is small in comparison to that of other sexual organs. Some great minds suggest that more education about it would help alleviate or even eliminate the social stigmas associated with the female body and sexual pleasure, such as, "The clitoris and vulva, in general, are unappealing. Female masturbation is taboo. Men should master and control women's orgasms."

❑ The Parts of the Clitoris and Their Functions

Clitoris

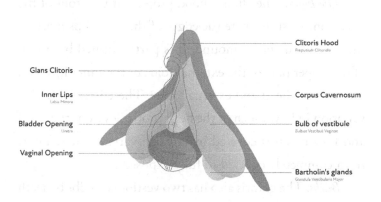

Clitoris Hood
Preputium Clitoridis

Glans Clitoris

Inner Lips
Labia Minora

Corpus Cavernosum

Bladder Opening
Urethra

Bulb of vestibule
Bulbus Vestibuli Vaginae

Vaginal Opening

Bartholin's glands
Glandula Vestibularis Major

When it comes to female genitalia, what we see is only an invitation to the hidden, bewildering wonders. Studies have identified eighteen parts in the clitoral network, many of which are invisible, but they highly contribute to female sexual pleasure. The clitoral body (may be referred to as the shaft or internal shaft), for example, is attached to the head and runs beneath the surface of the skin. It's a little pipe composed of spongy erectile tissue, extremely receptive to touch. It extends north from the head toward the mons pubis before forking and dividing like a wishbone or upside-down Y into two legs that flare downward, along the path of the inner lips and surrounding the two bulbs of erectile tissue—clitoral bulbs. Associated are the ureteral and perineal sponges, a network of nerves and blood vessels, the suspensory ligaments of the clitoris, and the pelvic floor muscle. The clitoral body or shaft supports the glans, and its shape can be seen and felt through the clitoral hood.

The hood. The clitoral hood projects at the front of the labia commissure where the edges of the outer lips meet, at the base of the pubic mound. It is partly formed by fusion of the upper part of the external folds of the inner lips, and it covers the head and external body. There is considerable variation in how much of the head protrudes from the hood and how much is covered by it. Such variation may range from completely covered to fully exposed.

Bulbs. The clitoris also has two vestibular bulbs beneath the skin of the labia minora at the vaginal entrance, which expand at the same time as the glans clitoris, to cap the ends of the corpora cavernosa. When engorged with blood, the bulbs cuff the vaginal opening and expand the vulva outward.

In pictures, all sexual organs look big. Even when we read their description and function, we picture everything big. We get the idea that the vulva is a vast territory in a woman's treasure land, but, in fact, an open hand can cover the entire vulva. An anatomical description and function of a female clitoral network is not only very confusing but also leaves the impression of the phenomenal matrix from here to China and back. When we go there and can't find something because it overlaps, we get frustrated.

Consider the following:

- The vagina is only three to five inches in a dormant stage.
- The clitoral head is the size of a pea (varying from 2 mm to 1 cm at 4–5 mm in both the transverse and longitudinal planes).
- The total clitoral length, including glans and body, is 4.3 mm.
- The clitoral body and crura together can be 10 cm (3.9 inches).

It's easily understood, then, that a woman's "down there" is a very tiny territory, yet I strongly hold to the saying, "Great things come in small packages," by the incredible amount of pleasure it generates. Research indicates that clitoral tissue extends into the vagina's anterior wall. No wonder every move we make down there is pleasurable!

11

Vagina

In a nonaroused state, the vagina is a compressed tube about three to five inches long, composed of muscle and lined with membranes, similar to the lining of the mouth. During arousal, a woman's vagina widens and opens to accommodate the penis, fingers, or sex toys. A "muscular tube leading from the vulva to the cervix of uterus in women and most mammals," the vagina is one of the greatest female reproductive organs. Its opening is partly covered by a membrane called the hymen. The vagina carries a variety of specialties, such as pleasure, allowing menstruation blood flow, and delivering a baby. Its skin—mucosa—is folded like an accordion (same as in our stomach), which allows for ballooning. This gives a vagina the ability to accommodate a variety of penises, fingers, tampons, sex toys, and baby deliveries and then return to its normal state. It has a rich network of blood flow, allowing pleasure and quick healing after injuries. Oh yes, it is moist and warm! And it drives us men crazy. And let's leave it at that.

Ignorance gave way to misconceptions and false descriptions of the vagina's activities and importance. Some people think a vagina is a never-ending narrow open space and that it only smells when it's infected. Thanks to science and female liberation, here are some truths of the matter:

Sizes and shapes. A 1996 study by Pendergrass, taken from the vaginas of thirty-nine Caucasian women, found the following:

o   Length: three to six inches (about the length of your hand)
o   Width: two to three inches
o   Introital: one to three inches

Studies have shown significant variations in size and shape of vaginas of women of different ethnicity, but there's no correlation between race and size or between race and the shape of the vagina. The vagina canal is three to six inches long but expands during sex and childbirth. Sexual arousal, for example, forces the cervix and uterus to lift, causing the upper two-thirds of the vagina to lengthen for penetration. If you feel a penis or sex toy hitting your cervix, your body isn't turned on for a full penetration, the thrusting is too deep, or a penis or toy is longer than average penis size (five to seven inches when erect).

As your vaginal canal and its opening stretches to allow a baby to pass through, your vagina will feel loose or dry or look wider afterward, but it should become tighter within a few days after childbirth and will return to its prebirth shape about six months after delivery. Although your vagina's appearance won't be the same, it'll be close.

Permanently stretched out. It's impossible for a vagina to be stretched out permanently. Vaginas are elastic; they're able to expand and snap back like rubber bands. Also, contrary to popular misconception, frequent sex or lack of it won't cause a vagina to lose its elasticity. Only childbirth and aging can cause that. Women who have had more than one vaginal birth are more likely to have weakened vaginal muscles, and aging can cause your vagina to stretch slightly and weaken the vaginal muscles, whether you've had children or not.

Pelvic floor muscles. Pelvic floor muscles are two layers of muscles located between the tailbone and the pubic bone to support the vagina and its opening and bladder and bowel continence, among other functions, such as orgasm. They contract three to fifteen times, instinctively, during an orgasm. A pelvic floor muscle that's too weak or torn, which can be caused by childbirth, leads to difficulty in getting an orgasm, or it can affect your sex drive. Too-tight pelvic floor muscles, resulting in muscle spasms, could lead to painful sex and pelvic pain.

The G-spot. There's no consistent evidence that the G-spot physically exists. In 1950, German physician Ernst Gutenberg suggested an area of the anterior vaginal wall was sensitive to touch and that stimulation of this area could bring orgasm. Not all agree. Therefore, debate about its existence is ongoing. The argument is that what is called the G-spot is an area, since arousing the area brings pleasure, and the spot is the clitoris shaft end.

In summary, it is what it is. Some women have brown or reddish labia, while others may have pink or purplish. Your genitals may also become darker when you're aroused, as blood flow to the area causes swelling, and the color of your clitoris and inner lips change. The only concern is if the changed color is a chronic purple, which could be the result of a yeast infection and the chronic irritation of the vulva, known as a lichen simplex. You should visit a doctor if you're worried about your vagina.

❑ **Your Vagina in Your Twenties**

o Strength: The ideal time for childbirth; it's a prime pelvic floor.

o Self: Don't put fragrance in your vagina.

o Sex: Your birth control may affect natural lubrication. During your twenties, your vagina doesn't struggle with natural lubrication unless you're on birth control pills, which can decrease it. If you notice a decrease, switch birth control. Lubricants help with painful tampon insertion and sexual intercourse. Sexual positions and discoveries should happen here. Play safely but as energetic as you can. Respect your vagina; avoid sexually transmitted diseases, but give it plenty of exercise. Train it right for the marathons ahead.

❑ Your Vagina in Your Thirties

o Strength: It's the ideal time to start Kegel training to keep your pelvic floor in great shape to support your orgasms. Your pelvic floor muscles are one of your body parts that you shouldn't wait until is broken to fix it. You'll learn more as you continue reading this book and others of this kind.

o Self: Practice mindfulness and communication.

o Sex: Use lube if you notice a decrease in lubrication. There's not much difference between sexual libido and stamina levels in your twenties and thirties, but they may have a temporary setback. Life circumstances are more pressing in your thirties as you deal with life's demands. The mortgage, kids, career, stress, and frustration can affect your libido and interfere with your sexuality.

❑ Your Vagina in Your Forties

o Strength: Ramp up on exercises for core muscles.

o Self: Take a probiotic for your vagina's health.

o Sex: Try new positions in the bedroom. Two common perimenopause symptoms may affect your sex life: a decrease in vaginal lubrication and vaginal dryness. Use a lubricant and allow plenty of time for foreplay and clitoral stimulation before intercourse. If vaginal dryness persists, your doctor can prescribe a topical estrogen cream.

Physically, your body is not the same as it was in your twenties. In other words, it's normal for sex to be accompanied by a few joint discomforts.

❑ Your Vagina in Your Fifties and Beyond

o   Strength: Increase Kegel exercises, and see your doctor for pain.

o   Self: Communicate changes to your partner and your doctor.

o   Sex: Increase the foreplay, and take it slow. As estrogen levels continue to drop, you may notice a decrease of vaginal lubrication. The internal vaginal tissues can become thin, fragile, and poorly lubricated, causing vaginal pain and bleeding with sexual intercourse. Fortunately, these symptoms tend to plateau and then disappear.

❑ Vaginal Discharge or Lubrication?

Contrary to what women might think (probably brainwashed by men), vaginal discharge is a normal phenomenon. It changes in amount, color, and consistency throughout a menstrual cycle. It can be clear or milky, and consistency may be creamy, sticky, or similar to that of egg whites, depending on what phase of your cycle you're in. Its amount varies between one and three milliliters in twenty-four hours (four milliliters—a completely soaked minipad—is considered normal). One of the many reasons a woman is lubricated, even when she's not aroused, is that secretions are part of the vagina's natural way of staying bad bacteria-free.

By the way, vaginal lubrication is not a sign of arousal—readiness for party. She could be wet solely because of the process of the vagina's self-cleaning. Alternately, she could be highly aroused but not lubricated. (Thanks, biology! Out of all the trouble we go through to read women, you gave us a double meaning down there.)

An unusual increase in discharge, a change in the odor of your vaginal discharge, or irritation or itchiness around your vagina are signs of vaginitis. These symptoms are caused by many things—douching, hygiene sprays, pregnancy, infection, or antibiotics—that throw off the balance of a healthy vagina; these also reflect the possibility of inflammation of the vagina, vulva, or cervix.

❑ **Scent and Odor**

First, let's clear the air. Scent is not smell. Scent is the product of the natural activities of the cells in our bodies; therefore, it's unique to each of us—our identity aroma—and, in general, it's a pleasant smell. Noticeable or not, we all have one. If you go down on a woman on a regular basis, and you don't know or don't miss the scent of her vagina, I may call you liar.

If there is an odor (bad smell) in the genital area, pay attention to personal hygiene. Like men, women sweat. A shower or bath or even engaging in what the French call "heart wash"—a quick, refreshing wash of the underarms and genital area—can get rid of unwanted odors. Many factors, however, contribute to the odor of a vagina. If you attend to personal hygiene and the unpleasant smell persists, it's time to see a doctor. You could be suffering from an infection. Bacterial vaginosis—in which a lack of lactobacilli creates an imbalance and allows anaerobic bacteria to accumulate—is the most common vaginal problem for women, ages fifteen to forty-four. It's estimated that one in three American women gets it, with a higher rate in black women. By the way, this is where the vaginal odor comparison to fish comes from, as these bacteria produce trimethylamine, the same substance that gives day-old fish its odor. Diet, vitamin deficiencies, medication, menstrual cycle, infections, hydration, alcohol, drugs, or tobacco can affect the smell and taste of a vagina. Unprotected sex can also affect a woman's smell because sperm is highly alkaline and raises the pH level of the vaginal ecosystem.

Some people believe women's genitals are as clean as a fresh carton of yogurt. Such a comparison is made because lactobacilli, a bacterium in yogurt, is also found in vaginal secretions. Some suggest that eating yogurt can alleviate infection and restore balance, although others say there is no food that will change the smell of your vagina. Antibiotics do restore balance.

In your twenties, especially in the age of social media, it's common to feel pressure to do something to improve your appearance. Your vagina is no exception. Honolulu Floral, for example, may be a great scent for your vagina, but it's a mistake that compromises your vaginal health. Your vagina is not meant to smell like a flower bouquet. Instead of fragranced products, use warm water and unscented soap to clean your vagina on a daily basis. Save the pumpkin-spice scent, for example, for your armpits.

Every woman smells and tastes different. Some are sweeter, others are a bit pungent, neutral, or nondescript. Sometimes, the differences are subtle; other times they are distinct. No woman smells or tastes consistently the same. Care about your odor, and your scent will care for itself.

❏ **Virginity**

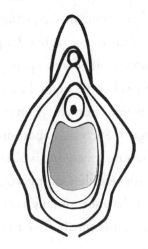

Society has made it impossible not to think of the hymen when we talk about virginity. Thankfully, misconceptions, bias, and prejudices are weakened and die by cultural changes and discoveries. What is the hymen anyway?

Contrary to what men have come up with—a way of valuing women; the magic cherry for which a woman must be honored when she allows a man to "pop it," therefore owing her a marriage, kids, happiness, love, and respect—the hymen is a thin layer of membranes surrounding the vaginal opening and is located about an inch from the vaginal entry. Most women have it. In children, the hymen commonly appears to be crescent-shaped, although many shapes are possible. During puberty, estrogen causes the hymen to change appearance and become very elastic. Variations of the postpubertal hymen range from thin and stretchy to thick and somewhat rigid. It can (but does not necessarily) rip or tear during first intercourse, which usually results in pain, and sometimes, mild temporary bleeding or spotting can occur.

Sources differ on how common tearing or bleeding is during first intercourse. Science doesn't know why women have hymens or what the function is. Some say the hymen protects the vagina from harmful elements, such as bacteria. I agree with that, as the hymen lives when a girl doesn't know much about taking care of her genitalia. Because the skin of vagina is very sensitive and vulnerable, even a small amount of dirt in the vagina can cause an inflammatory reaction. Somehow, myths, bias, and prejudice (of course, men!) have attached the hymen to virginity as inseparable twins. Here are some of the myths:

Using a tampon affects virginity. Virginity is lost by sexual penetration, period. It doesn't matter how many objects travel through or pound your vagina; you are a virgin until the day you have intercourse. Virginity is, after all, "the state of never having had sexual intercourse." Sexual intercourse is "the physical activity of sex, usually describing the act of a man putting his penis inside a woman's vagina"; "sexual contact between individuals involving the insertion of a man's erect penis into a women's vagina"; "sexual intercourse is a sexual activity typically involving the insertion of a penis into the vagina for sexual pleasure, reproduction, or both"; "sexual intercourse ... involving penetration of the vagina by the penis." I rest my case.

Many women—virgins or not—use tampons to absorb menstrual flow or excessive vaginal discharge. A tampon can only stretch or tear the hymen of some women.

Your partner can confirm your virginity by looking at your hymen. This is a big pile of crap. In general, girls lose their virginity in their late teens or early adulthood. At that age, we don't know much (nor do we care) about a woman's sexual anatomy. We only look for the vaginal opening and rush to penetration. If there's blood, the misconceptions bring a smile and greater satisfaction because we believe she was a virgin. Furthermore, not even a gynecologist can tell if a girl is virgin by looking at her hymen, so how can an ordinary man?

A gynecological checkup might affect virginity. The only way this can be true is if a doctor uses his penis for examination, which would be a "fucking" instead of an examination.

A hymen is the seal of a woman's worthiness. In certain communities, important cultural significance is given to the hymen because of its association with a woman's virginity. In those cultures, an intact hymen is highly valued at marriage, as it's believed this is proof of virginity. Some women undergo *hymenorrhaphy*, a surgical restoration of hymen, for this reason. Do you see what men's ignorance can make women go through? To take virginity as the seal of worthiness is an absurd idea that only ignorant men can have, and they should be ashamed. The state of the hymen is not a reliable indicator of virginity. Yet virginity testing remains a practice.

A virgin bleeds when she loses her virginity. Possibly, not necessarily. Vaginal blood can be present if a virgin had a hymen that was very stiff and that tore during penetration. Also, if she wasn't lubricated enough, she could see blood as a result of friction. I've had of those days that stick forever— great, long sexual sessions. Doggy style was the endgame. As we walked to the store, I felt as light as a feather and as happy as a clam. I was proud of myself. I put my arm around her shoulder and whispered, "I want it again."

She said, "No. You've had enough already. And my body hurts. Actually, I saw blood."

Did that mean I'd just taken her virginity? Hell, no! She had kids. Poor lubrication, inexperience, and rough sex are some contributing factors in a virgin (or a mother) bleeding during sex.

A virgin bleeds during the first intercourse as the hymen breaks. The hymen thins over time and might recede to nothing. On the other side of the river, some women have a hymen that stretches easily. In this case, it would accommodate a large penis or sex toys without giving out any blood. Despite the possibility, bleeding from the hymen is debatable, as vagina walls could be responsible for the bleeding.

The hymen is the only indicator of virginity. Many girls do not have hymens but might not have inserted anything into their vaginas. Are they not virgins? What about the girls who have had tons of sexual intercourse and have their hymens just about as new as before their first sexual intercourse? Are they virgins? Then, only the woman's true words can settle the issue of her virginity.

The hymen covers the vagina. The hymen restricts the opening of the vagina. In rare cases, it covers the vagina; this is called *imperforated hymen*, a congenital disorder, and it requires surgery so menstrual blood can flow. There is also a *septate hymen*, a hymen with a band that causes two small vaginal openings, making it very difficult or impossible to insert even a tampon into the vagina.

You always know when your hymen breaks. This one is as screwed up as the others. Your hymen can "break" before having sex for the first time. Horseback riding, cycling, gymnastic sessions, insertion of tampons, or masturbation can break a hymen unnoticeably.

Even with our opening our minds and understanding women's genitalia and biology—thanks to female sexual empowerment and freedom from male dominance—we still take virginity as a treasure. Some cultures demand that husbands return "disgraceful wives" to their families. Ignorance has given the guilty verdict to so many innocent women who are virgins.

❑ Losing Your Virginity

Deana was beautiful and enthusiastic. Her behavior with boys—flirting, playing hard to get, provocative and sometimes sexually expressive moves—was that of a teenager who wanted desperately to lose virginity. Opportunity knocked when she found herself home alone for the evening. She called her friends to come over to chill. They all had fun, and when they talked about boys and sex, her friends encouraged her to call a boy. She did. Her friends warmed up the atmosphere and spread love in the air. Deana started fooling around, as usual, except her focus was on losing virginity that night.

Somehow, everything was different. They were making out, but she was not at ease or enjoying it as usual. She turned on the stereo and played her favorite songs to soothe and calm her spirit, but she still wasn't feeling it. The boy, although not virgin, wasn't experienced enough to put Deana at ease; he left shortly afterward.

Her friends cheered, "Go, girl! Go, girl!"

"I told you that shit was about to be no more," one of the girls said, except those words brought tears to Deana's eyes. A quick plan worked out fine.

To prove not all girls will lose their virginity as planned or wished, nor will the enjoyment be the same, here's another example:

Susana was the fifth of the eight children and grew up under strict house rules. At eighteen, fresh from high school graduation, she got a job at a government enterprise as a clerk. This new step in her life meant freedom to be with a man without having to hide from her brothers or answer questions at home. Hot, beautiful, and full of desire to explore the wild side, her life was taking a turn.

One of her coworkers was a father in his early thirties. He was single but attached to a couple of women, who were raising his kids. His circumstances weren't as much of a problem for Susana as his ugliness. His determination was strong, but Susana was out of his league—until one summer afternoon.

With an abundance of love in the air, after everybody

had left the workplace, a dark corner of the building was about to witness the end of something special and the beginning of a terrific thing. The fear of being caught sped up the action, but it was enough time to celebrate pleasure.

The tenderness of the kisses and fondling started slowly but quickly began to build up. Her body temperature was warm, and her heart was pounding faster and was unusually intense. Her sea-blue silk blouse was off, and the bright-white bra, which gave her breasts firmness and support, was about to be off unusually fast. The yellow shirt that covered Lorenzo's slim upper body came off as well. Susana's breasts, now free from the bra and standing firm on her slender chest, were something beyond wonderful, ready for ecstasy. They didn't need the bra to keep them sturdy. Lorenzo looked at them in amazement; they were beautifully desirable, just as he had imagined. Looking at them alone brought him the hardest erection he could ever remember. He raised his hands and touched them. He lifted them just a little bit, squeezed them gently for a couple of seconds, and dipped his head down to suck on them, one after another. Susana looked down to witness his action while enjoying the erotic sensation.

Lorenzo kept switching from minor bites and pulling on her nipples to sucking a good amount of her breast into his mouth. She raised his head and went for tongue play. Lorenzo dipped her head to the side to respond better to her desire, while his other arm kept her body pressed against his.

Each play and touch seemed more powerful and desirable and made her body desire something more. Quickly, he dropped his pants and underwear to his ankles to free his penis. He pulled her closer, and she offered no resistance. He lifted her black mini skirt, removed her underwear, and guided the action.

The head of his penis made rough landings, but the hymen or something was resisting the entry. Susana wasn't sure about the right moves to make the entry easier, but she knew that in seconds, her world would never be the same. The pricking came strong enough to break something free. She didn't fall flat; she stood up almost straight to accept the strokes. She responded mostly with moans and groans, increasingly louder and more intense, and then she exploded in what seemed to be her first orgasm on her first vaginal penetration.

Lost in his arms, still having occasional shudders, she waited to regain her composure. A minute went by in this delicate after-sex moment. She was back on earth now. Gently, she pushed her body from him. She raised her right hand to clear the tears before she kissed his lips, tenderly.

I know Susana. She never dreamed of losing her virginity to someone older than she was or in that way. I told her of many cases of women losing their virginity that didn't happen according to plan. She said, "Don't get me wrong. It was an incredible experience!"

There's not a unanimous definition of virginity. For

some, being a virgin means you haven't had any kind of penetrative sex—vaginal, anal, or oral. Others may define virginity as never engaging in vaginal penetration with a penis, despite having had other types of sex, including oral stimulation and anal penetration. A popular acceptance of virginity is never having had sex, but its ambiguity leaves you lost.

Well, none of those definitions matters. What matters is that *you* decide when you're ready to lose your virginity, be comfortable with that decision, and be educated about it. Let's say that losing your virginity is sexual intercourse for the first time. Rushing can bring a sour taste to your mouth, including unwanted pregnancy and disease. Don't feel pressured by your peers who are no longer virgins. Don't simply do what others have done to fit in the group. I believe that eighteen years of age is reasonable for losing virginity, but this is your sole decision, and you should know the facts.

It can be painful, but that also varies from person to person and depending on the circumstances. If you have your first vaginal penetration in a rush, it could hurt a lot. If you have had anal penetration with a penis, it shouldn't be painful; your body already knows what having sex entails. Vaginal penetration will be just another sexual act with a penis. If you masturbated on a regular basis and used a dildo and vibrators, your vagina already has been stretched out to accommodate a penis. If you never inserted anything inside you, and you want to avoid pain, long foreplay for natural lubrication, as well as use of lubricants, will help with friction. With that said, to minimize discomfort with your first sexual penetration, masturbate frequently with the objects that resemble a penis. This will stretch your vagina and get your body used to responding to penetration arousal. If you are drunk, the booze and anxiety will suppress the pain. There are consequence here, since when you're drunk, your thinking is impaired; you could engage in unsafe sexual acts, which could land an STI/STD and pregnancy in your lap. Be aware, and be smart.

To this day, we are "the man" if we take a girl's virginity. The boys are still not washing blood off their penises when they have sex with a virgin girl who bled, as proof to their friends. The myth persists that once you take a girl's virginity, she'll never forget you and that she'll give it to you forever. Girls do take virginity as a treasure. Many girls cried when they lost their virginity, and from a good standpoint, that is understandable. Having intercourse for the first time is a big deal. It's the transition from girlhood to womanhood. Most girls take virginity as something special, but it's gone in two seconds—and forever. I respect that, but I would like you to have a different approach to your first vaginal penetration. Do your best to make it a celebration worth remembering. You might go through temporary physical and emotional pain for the enduring pleasure. After all, you've just opened the gates of paradise to enjoy one of the best rewards God has ever given us—sexual penetration.

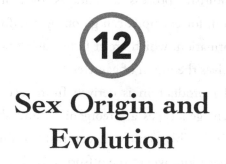

Sex Origin and Evolution

What is a journey that can't be too short or it's madness and can't be too long or it's frustrating, and our not having it drives us insane?

Sex!

The origin of sex is difficult to prove. Researchers have focused on the persistence of sexual reproduction over time to support their theories. It can be traced to early *prokaryotes* (microscopic single-celled organisms) around two billion years ago, when bacteria began exchanging genes via conjugation, transformation, and transduction. These processes are distinct from true sexual reproduction but share some basic similarities. They are the foundations for true sex that arrived in the last eukaryotic ancestors.

Prevalence of sexual reproduction by natural selection in a highly competitive world has been one of the major mysteries of biology because asexual reproduction and hermaphroditism possess advantages over it. Asexual reproduction, for example, can go on by budding, fission, or spore formation, which are at faster rates than sexually, which involves the union of gametes.

Sexual reproduction is derived from recombination, where parent genotypes are reorganized and shared with the offspring. This stands in contrast to single-parent asexual replication, where the offspring is always identical to the parents (barring mutation) and brings no variety or distinction. Before that, the adaptation process, where genes would change from one generation to the next (genetic mutation) was very slow and random.

Sex solved that problem. It evolved as an extremely efficient way for producing variation, and this had the major advantage of enabling organisms to adapt to changing environments. Diversification in the phylogenetic tree happens much faster via sexual reproduction than it does by asexual reproduction. Also, sexual reproduction offers significant fitness advantages because despite the twofold cost of sex (spending energy looking for a mate and spending lots of energy during sexual penetration), it dominates among multicellular forms of life. By the way, current sexual reproduction comes with fourfold cost, as we add money and sexually transmitted diseases to it.

Now that you have a notion of the origin and evolution of sex, let's have some real talk.

Penetrative Sex

Chances are that you've never pondered on the fact that the moment you won the sperm marathon—it penetrated the egg—the second and most important phase of your greatness began; on the day you were born, the third phase of your greatness began.

The world, your family, and your parents welcomed you but weren't sure about your capabilities to deliver what would be expected of you yet. At the beginning of your puberty— the day a girl experiences her first period, and a boy has his first ejaculation—the fourth phase of your greatness began, with a list of obligations, with procreation at the top of the list, as you became the product of procreation, ready to procreate. When you became a parent, you proved your worthiness to the world, your family, and your parents.

Penetrative sex essence is the continuity of our kind and the expansion of the family tree, in which you are an active participant. This type of sex is always on your mind because it helps you shine as a positive contributor to the cause.

Procreation can be done first by sexual intercourse. A relationship makes procreation possible, easy, and more rewarding. We can procreate without relationships, but all types of sex are celebrated better in a relationship. Evolution has taught us that each can survive alone, but both combined seem to hit the jackpot because procreation in the natural way is a divine mandate, and relationships are important steps in social integration and foster the way to populate.

With sexual penetration ingrained in our DNA, we think of sex as vagina/penis penetration first. This is another trick of biology, but penetrative sex encompasses anal sex, irrumation, and mammary sex. Any of these are bound by the same particularity, which is the duration of penetration. If it lasts more than fifteen minutes, it's considered too long; less than seven minutes is short, and less than three minutes is too short. There are many contributing factors, however, in the duration of a sexual session that includes penetration, and the satisfaction is not dictated by how long he keeps his penis hard like a rock and pounds you like a sex machine would. Sadly, that's how men, the owners of penises, think, and this thinking only brings worries about coming before she does, to the detriment of fun.

You should ignore this nonsense. It is worth it, though, to learn and practice the duration-of-penetration control tricks, yet be aware that regardless of your expertise, you will never be able to control fully the duration of your penetration because the complexity of sexuality takes away your full control. The following are popular tricks that can help lengthen your sexual penetration but without guarantee or consistency. It is your responsibility to discover what works best and is safest for you.

- Avoid excessive alcohol. Doctors recommend two drinks before the action.
- Masturbate before the party.
- Be fit and healthy.
- Don't start penetration when your arousal level is high (close to orgasm).
- Start slowly and gradually increase the speed and intensity.
- Don't fantasize right from the start.
- Distract your mind when you feel the arousal increasing rapidly.
- Slow down to almost stopping; then stop without pulling out. Kiss and caress her. Give tender bites to her nipples, and do whatever is appropriate for the moment, briefly, and restart thrusting slowly.
- Change positions frequently.
- Stop, pull out, and briefly do something else.
- Pull out and squeeze the base of your penis to halt ejaculation (some experts do not recommend doing this).

- Use desensitizing condoms, wipes, and sprays. (There could be side effects in using these products.)
- Use over-the-counter enhancement pills.

In addition to these moves, you can read materials related to this subject, or consult a sexologist or your doctor.

It's worth noting that lasting for a long time is not the main ingredient for satisfactory sexual penetration. As long as you are healthy, sane, and committed to the work at hand, your penetrative sex of any kind will be pleasurable and satisfactory. There may be cause to worry if your erection consistently declines, as that could be a sign of an underlying problem.

Erection is a must for sexual penetration to happen. I believe that sexual penetration was designed to last three to seven minutes, as this is how long it takes a man to ejaculate in a vagina. Either biological evolution or human greed has made it seem, to some extent, that when it comes to sex, the longer time is better. Sure, sometimes we want it to last all night long, but we can make a glory out of the three to seven minutes or less. A quickie is shorter than that but does wonders!

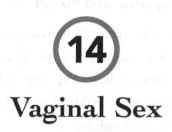

14

Vaginal Sex

We already know that the vagina is not the queen of sexual pleasure, but only through it can we conceive naturally. We're brainwashed into believing that sex without vaginal penetration is not sex and that no other sexual act is more pleasurable than vaginal penetration. Indeed, the feeling of having someone inside you or being inside someone is phenomenal. Some individuals have killed and died for it. We can have all sorts of sex, but we don't feel satisfied until we have vaginal penetration. The statistical average of a men having sexual thoughts is nineteen times a day; for women, it's twelve times a day. (I believe the numbers are low and that woman don't fall behind like that.) This is not specific, but I assume it focused on vaginal penetration, even if only for the endgame. When we refer to sexual dissatisfaction, we mean vaginal penetration. We can't escape the biological trap. Take note and have fun with a variety of sexual intercourse.

❏ Sex, Making Love, and Rough Sex

Similar to tree branches being part of the same trunk but very distinct in nature, this trio is a distinct triplet bonded by the same ribbon. The way each sexual act is performed is what sets sex, making love, and rough sex apart from one another. Let's indulge.

❏ Sex

When you're having fun under the sheets, where anything goes, you are having sex. Everything happens naturally. You fool around, caress, rub, kiss, and then go down on your partner while he fingers you, or you engage in sixty-nine (mutual oral sex) for a short time. Then penetration starts and goes on for about five to seven minutes. Both of you come or she comes first. You've just had sex. There is no novelty or ceremony of any kind. It's more like two people having sex ordinarily to fill a biological demand. It could also be a way to relaxation—a stress and frustration relief.

When we were drunk, horny, on a one-night stand, or we only had time for a quickie, we had sex. It can bring the benefits of sexual activity, in general, but we're prone to becoming bored with sex sooner than with making love or rough sex. Sex carries little or no intimacy, love, romance, or emotional bond. It's like running or any other physical activity, except more pleasurable. Men, in general, like sexual activities with no strings attached. (No, we aren't dogs— maybe a little. It's all the work of biology.) People who are comfortable with having sex without sharing any emotional attachments are the first victims of sexual dissatisfaction. Newer generations fall prey to this reality, brought to them by female sexual empowerment, the media, the internet (Instagram, Snapchat), and pornography. Chris Rock mentioned this in one of his stand-up comedy routines—that women now have sex fast and then leave.

Yet sex can be fun, emotional, and interesting. It all depends on you. In fact, make-up sex can be very emotional and intense, with powerful orgasms.

Make-up sex. You might know how intense and pleasurable make-up sex can be. Here's a story from a friend of mine:

> I was single, going through some rough waters. God sent a woman my way for rescue, but things were not moving quite smoothly. We had been dating for two months. Up to that point, we had not enjoyed ourselves fully. We had had chances for nothing other than sex. She came over, and I couldn't perform, once again. She got upset and decided to end our relationship. I blamed stress and frustration and no foreplay, but she had already made [up] her mind. I was sobbing as she put her handbag on her shoulder and walked to the door. I

frenetically followed her. She leaned against the door, speechless and looking straight into my eyes. I read that as a request for a goodbye kiss. She raised her head to reach my lips. I was counting on a wet kiss, even though my face was soaked in tears. The emotion was very high in both of us, and it led to a long, intense, and passionate kiss. Our body temperatures were boiling up at lightning speed, with emotions traveling at supersonic speed.

I was hearing the roar of her soul through her moaning and groaning as the adrenaline rush had taken over. I was on fire, and so was my penis. Suddenly, I was inside her, for the first time in a standing-up position. I furiously stroked her hard and fast. We were on the third floor, but I'm pretty sure people on the first could hear us. Lost in ecstasy, I didn't care, nor did she. Nothing else mattered at that moment. The speed and intensity of my strokes increased to crazy—we were coming hard. In a burst of ecstasy, I felt her legs trembling as she pressed on my shoulders. It was the best we ever had.

❑ Making Love

Making love is sweet! It has passion, romance, desire, caressing, cuddling, looking into each other's eyes, holding each other tight, and staying there forever. It's settling, beautiful, fulfilling, satisfactory, appreciative, and transcendent—a travel to the moon and back. It has sensual, gentle, rough, and crazy sexual acts. It's the queen of all kings and queens of sex and the greatest way of showing love and appreciation. Sadly, we don't make love as frequently as we should because it is demanding and time-consuming— even exhausting at times. We can't have it under pressure. Our minds, bodies, and spirits must be there and be in sync. Since we have other ways to satisfy our sexual desires, we save the best for last, but we often forget the best. What a waste of good wine! What a shame and disgrace to humankind!

Women rightly want to be loved, cared for, and sexed right (and hard sometimes), but they are empty without making love. Men's priority to their macho man is the first reason women get fed up with sexual dissatisfaction and call it quits. We push making love to the back burner because we can be stupid, ignorant jackasses. Every generation faces obstacles to being real in bed—romantic, loving, caring, and a deliverer—but we could do better.

Let's take a second look at social norms and taboos and understand that men are women's servants, with the obligation to service them right, especially in bed, not the opposite. Love them and show them how much in bed. Yes, many women will despise us after we show love, caring, and appreciation. They want to be screwed rough and move on. That's how they are wired or have twisted themselves for sexual joy. They are the exceptions to the rules. In my view, women who throw away love, care, appreciation, respect, and dignity are crazy or are suffering from a psychological disturbance.

Reach into your mind with a couple of drinks and then act on the sexual inspiration.

The time: Prepare the field for the game when she's ovulating, as this is the best time for great sexual satisfaction. Her body and mind are in sync and ready for procreation. Don't start the preparation ten minutes before you both are in bed. Any good sexual adventure is better when planned miles and days ahead. Start with creative imagination or keep sex in your mind. Flirt and send texts and emails that carry direct and indirect messages of sex, love, and appreciation.

The mood. No arguments. She rules; she can't be wrong. Be there, be there, be there—period. Romance her with extra care in a way that makes her feel like a million dollars. Small, meaningful actions speak loudly. Flowers are great. If you can afford it, jewelry—not necessarily expensive because this is not a one-time action—with flowers is the best, but you should know what takes her to glory.

Cooperation. Speak your mind and get a "signed

contract." She will enthusiastically sign and follow it when most articles are in her favor.

Location: Habit brings comfort, but it kills innovation and attracts boredom. Hotel, motel, friend's house, cruise, and exotic vacations are some great venues for a making-love adventure.

Stay ahead of the game. Anticipate her desires and fulfill them. Hire a maid for the day, and oversee the housekeeping, laundry, and food shopping. Detail her car and replace the floor mats. If you live slightly above poverty, save $600 in cash, and send her to shop without you. And finally, repeat what worked, and find new ways of arousing the pathway to making love. Never get discouraged when you fall short.

The action. As she washes dishes or fixes the window curtains, stand behind her, hug her belly, and kiss her neck. If you have a boner, let her feel it, just that. I am pretty sure she will comment on that. Give her a scoop of ice cream or her favorite chocolate bar. Use your imagination to keep the mood going strong. Take a bath together for relaxation, and focus on her needs. Dry her body and kiss her neck or shoulders as you leave the bathroom.

Don't get in the bedroom, slam the door shut, dim the lights, and put your plan into action. Let the imagination flow without disrupting your intentions. Say you want to enjoy each other for one hour. Don't let five minutes of foreplay bring your arousal to inevitable penetration. Tame your anxiety and desires.

After a long-enough time of fooling around, start with a relaxing massage to her favorite soothing songs. As she lies on her stomach, massage her legs, back, shoulders, and neck. Caress her hair, kiss her body tenderly, and keep skin contact continuous. As she is flat on her back, massage her chest and around her breasts. Connect to each other by French kissing while you rub her vulva with the palm of your hand before inserting your index finger into her vagina (not deeply), or simply tease her vaginal entrance. Kiss her entire body as you slowly travel to her vulva.

Give her all you've got for cunnilingus, and stay focused on her enjoyment, not your needs. Patience, slowness, gentleness, and tenderness are now the name of the game. Don't rush your moves to her orgasm. Keep her arousal on a slow, steady pace to save penetration. You're here to show love, care, and appreciation, not your abilities to make her have multiple orgasms by your penis and fingers alone. Stay with your tongue play on her vulva. Use your hands to caress her upper body again and stop at her breasts. Caress them and play with the nipples. Ease the tongue play to a stop when her pleasure intensifies. Come up and kiss her passionately. If she doesn't like to be kissed after cunnilingus, skip the kiss. Either way briefly rub your penis over her vulva, or hold your penis in your hand for guidance, rub the head up and down her lips, and do whatever feels right. Penetrate her slowly, if she hasn't taken you inside of her yet.

Start with shallow and slow strokes. Gradually increase the speed and depth of your thrust. Hold her tight with every move. Don't rush to come or bring her to orgasm. Change positions and stay connected. Today, missionary and the woman on top are the main menu for the endgame. These two positions allow for the closest body contact. Use your penis to stroke her vagina, your tongue to French kiss her, and your hands to caress her body at the same time. She eventually will pick up the vibe, if she hasn't yet. Take what comes as an endgame. I would be surprised if she didn't have multiple orgasms.

❑ Rough Sex

Rough sex is any sexual act dominated by penetration, where the level of physical activity is equal to a torturous workout, except it is pleasurable. It's such a thrill and is a measuring tool of our sexual potential in action. It's empowering, even if only temporarily. It's an addictive misconception that we can't sober up.

Beware: both the man and woman can pass out, have a heart attack, or die from rough sex. These extremes are usually associated with factors such as poor health and sex under heavy influence of alcohol or drugs.

Normal rough. During this sex act, we usually take a little time on arousal. The mind is already set for the vigorous actions of heavy and prolonged vagina-pounding in various positions. It can be equal to a hard physical activity for a man with a woman who enjoys receiving. Even with women who participate actively during sex—all women should do that—men get the hardest parts of the game. In general, women participate briefly and put themselves in the best position to be penetrated hard and fast.

Influenced rough. Booze and drugs are useful in many aspects of life, from feeling good to saving lives. They have been great players in sex as popular substances that make you last all night long. Women, in general, don't like sex with drunk men. I've heard, "They never come! They get drunk to kill a woman."

A few years ago, I was on vacation in Cape Verde. My brother-in-law had hooked me up for a round of fun. Moments before showdown, he advised me to take shots of rum "and then give it to her." Beyoncé condoned it with her song "Drunk in Love." It's ironic that alcohol, according to science, brings erection problems, such as decreasing hardness and sustainability, but it is one of the most popular rough-sex boosters. Enhancement pills like Viagra are the next most popular.

Joshua heard of a girl bragging about her lust and complaints of dissatisfaction. He went fishing and caught an opportunity. He was young and powerful, yet he took Viagra. He says, "It was straight-up sex. My dick was like a steel. I destroyed her pussy. When I was done, she couldn't walk. I didn't like the feeling of my dick hard like a steel and taking forever to come, but the mission was accomplished."

The intensity and speed of penetration during rough sex drive a man to sooner-than-usual ejaculation. The fun will be short, and the woman may not come. Enhancements solve this problem but not without consequences. Beware of the popular use of sexual enhancement pills throughout different age groups to avoid being a victim, especially if you have health problems, such as cardiovascular disease or any heart issues. It's still a misconception that a man must "give it to her hard all night long," or he's a loser. This misconception has driven many men to rely heavily on illegal sex drugs. And for a new vagina, this seems to be a mandate. It's all good if tragedy hasn't shown its face, but remember that tragedy doesn't send a notice of its arrival. You should reach for what floats your boat, if it's safe, but don't abuse what you may live without. Tackle ignorance with knowledge, and enjoy rough sex without fears or concerns.

The following story attests that rough sex can come to you naturally. And you can make it happen without assistance that carries consequences.

Out of nowhere—by-chance rough. This is one of the best—it comes unannounced. Many times, we start a sex act without a road map. Then, it all escalates to a savage power within. I like this rough the best. In general, both of you go crazy, and you don't understand it. Your minds take over your senses, and suddenly, here you are, both of you going insane and screwing.

I had it once. I was exhausted after I came. I didn't crash. Instead, I pulled myself out and lay down on the bed, but that was uncomfortable. I walked around the room, and that, too, was uncomfortable. I lay down on my back, arms stretched out, facing the ceiling. That was comfortable. I was breathing heavily, not tired, just out of myself. She had already hit the shower in a rush for a cooling off and taking the sweat away. When she returned from the shower, she thought I'd passed out.

"Are you OK?" she asked me.

Half asleep, I said, "I'm OK. It's just that … that was crazy."

"I thought you liked it," she said.

"I did!" I replied. I just haven't come like that in a very long time."

That memory stayed fresh for days.

Favorite positions, pros and cons. Doggy style is by far the most suitable for rough sex. It allows freedom of action. It's better when she's down on all fours at the edge of the bed, with you standing firm on the floor, penetrating her. To kill boredom and avoid fatigue, you can vary doggy positions to kneeling on the bed. Let her take charge, while you take a breath and then respond to her, thrusting. Still behind her, put your arms behind your back, elbows straight, and thrust as if you're using your lap to throw her ass up in the air. You can also move from here to being on your knees to free your hands for assistance, such as slapping her butt cheeks, caressing her breasts, stimulating her clitoris, pulling her hair, or grabbing her by the shoulders to rock her toward your lap for harder, deeper thrusting.

There will be times when you'll want to give her the option of using the headboard or wall for support. Things can happen fast and get brutal during rough sex. Gentle is out of sight, out of mind. When we're approaching intensive orgasm, the instinctive reaction is to grab her with both hands by waist for a speedy thrust and loud body slap. Holding on to something for protection is a good idea. You've seen smart porn girls protecting themselves against head bangs. The chances are, they've suffered from them.

Here's a friend's story:

> Once, my ex-girlfriend and I hit it on the bathroom floor in a cowgirl. When we were coming, I instinctively thrusted her hard, and she hit her head on the wall. There were no bruises or blood. I said sorry, and we both laughed, but I knew it hurt. We were not even going hard at it!

Are there more consequences than other forms of penetration? Of course! Rough sex increases the chance of pregnancy. The intensity of the action makes it hard to pull out before ejaculating inside her. The heat of the moment comes with strong and uncontrollable thrusts, and the strong orgasm that usually accompanies it hypnotizes us to stay inside her during ejaculation. Even after we come, we could still thrust as hard as we can. Also, the intensity of vagina-pounding increases the odds of condom rupture.

When having sex with someone for the first time, for example, we suffer the anxiety of premature ejaculation. We're concerned about doing a bad job, which pushes us into drinking alcohol and/or taking drugs to give her a good sexual experience. The problem is, when we are under the influence, we last longer. Her vagina could be dry, but she won't care or even feel the friction. Reason number one for why the party is over—she sees blood. The tears on her vaginal walls are a refuge for infectious bacteria. If she's not under the influence but is concerned about rejection or falling short of expectations, she could participate too actively and suffer the consequence later.

Benefits. Rough sex is great. You both can get an intense orgasm, and she can get euphoric multiple orgasms. It's the greatest release of muscle tension, relaxation, and a great sense of accomplishment, self-esteem, and self-worth. If you want to get pregnant, rough sex during ovulation could help.

Rough sex is a sexual act that brings heightened satisfaction. It entails penetration. Penetration is the only natural form by which a man impregnates a woman—an opportunity to spread his seeds of procreation, which have been written in his DNA. This is the main reason vaginas are very addictive. Rough sex is physically challenging.

That's the reason we can't do it every time we have sex—because the higher the intensity of the action, the greater the chances of a strong orgasm. A stronger orgasm accompanied by ejaculation allows a man to powerfully spray his semen farther inside a women's vagina, thus reducing the traveling distance to the eggs—a divine design. How smart! Even though rough sex is not the most rewarding sexual activity (which is not to say it can't be), and it's an energy killer, we brag about it. It makes us feel worthy as a man or woman. It makes us walk upright, chin up, a smile on our faces, and a spring in our steps. It makes men say to themselves, "I am the man!" It makes women act as if they rule the world (they do).

Rough sex gives physical and biological satisfaction and benefits like no other. It has gained miles with feminine independence and sexual liberation, where one-night stands and "friends with benefits" have been popularized. Both women and men like it. Please have it as often and as safely as you can.

❑ Irrumation

Also referred to as the sexual technique of thrusting the penis between the thighs of a partner (intercrural sex), irrumation is a type of oral sex in which someone thrusts his penis into another person's mouth, in contrast to fellatio, where the penis is being orally excited by a fellator. Therefore, the difference lies mainly in which partner takes the active role. Sadly, we leave irrumation on the back burner for two reasons. First, it doesn't bring much excitement. It's a treasured land we can explore in two minutes and have nothing else to do for the rest of the day. Second, irrumation originally was a form of rape and disgracing someone. Wikipedia describes it as,

> A form of oral sex in which someone thrusts their penis into another person's mouth, often with the intention of inducing gag reflex and forced vomiting … Is strictly a form of oral rape in which a man forces his penis into someone else's mouth, inducing vomiting for sexual gratification, and as a form of humiliation and degradation.

I know ignorant jackasses who embrace irrumation as a humiliating and degrading sexual act, instead of mutual pleasure. John Doe Q once told me and his friends, "I was screwing her mouth as hard as I could. Later, she asked me if I was trying to hurt her, and I said no. But I was!" (Good for you, asshole.)

During a phone argument, the other person said to me, "I will *fuck* your mother in the mouth!"

I am pretty sure you've heard stories like these.

Does that mean a woman wouldn't enjoy irrumation, or that we should leave it alone? Of course not! The tissue in the mouth is similar to that in vagina, and the mouth is nice and warm too. Human lips and tongue are filled with millions of nerve endings. They are aroused during oral sex, and they induce sexual thoughts. Tell me that you can watch a woman eating a banana, licking ice cream, or sucking on her thumb and never imagine having oral sex with her, and I might point to a liar.

Let's explore sexual pleasure and use our discoveries more often, without bias, taboos, and prejudice.

❑ Mammary Intercourse

Breast penetration, or mammary intercourse, is a sex act where a man thrusts his penis between a woman's breasts to simulate sexual penetration. It may be used as an alternative to a hand job. It is not fantasy or pornography propaganda. It's a widespread fact on a sex menu. An ex-sister-in-law lamented that her small breasts took away the possibility for mammary intercourse. Research shows its popularity and its slang terms—*paizuri* in Japan; titty-fucking, tit-job, or tit-fuck in the USA; tit wank or French fuck in England, with the latter term dating as far back as the 1930s.

Breasts are sensitive to touch, as they're packed with nerve endings. Studies have shown that the parts in the brain that respond to the stimulation of erogenous zones react when the breasts are stimulated. During sexual arousal, breast size increases, venous patterns across the breasts become more visible, and nipples harden. Stimulation of the nipples initiates the production of oxytocin, a hormone that creates pleasurable sensations throughout the genital area. Some women achieve an orgasm from nipple stimulation— nipplegasm—which belies reports that men get greater pleasure than women from female breast stimulation.

Anal Sex

Despite taboos, anal sex is growing in popularity among all ages. In a national survey, 36 percent of women and 44 percent of men reported that they've had anal sex with an opposite partner. Anal penetration has been recorded in gorillas, orangutans, some members of the genus Macaca, squirrel monkeys, and spider monkeys. Cases of anal penetration with fingers have been reported among orangutans.

And there you have it! We do it, and other animals do it and not just with a penis. Therefore, anal sex is the inserting of a penis, finger, or sex toy into the anus for sexual pleasure. However, it carries potential risks that may not be present in vaginal or oral sex. For example, the anus lacks the lubricant the vagina has to reduce discomfort and friction-related skin injuries. Also, the rectum's lining is thinner than that of vagina. The lack of lubrication and thinner tissues increase the risk of friction tears in the anus and rectum. Some of these tears may be very small but still expose the skin.

Because stool that naturally contains bacteria passes through the rectum and anus, bacteria can invade the skin through these tears, thus increasing the risk of anal abscesses, a skin infection that usually requires treatment.

Precautions to prevent the skin from tearing include the following:

- Stimulate the anus sufficiently before penetration.
- Use water-based lubricant to minimize friction-related tears.
- Slow thrust until she's well lubricated.
- Slow down if it's uncomfortable, and stop if it's painful.
- Avoid spermicides, as that can increase the risk of anal irritation.

Because anal sex can increase the risk of sexually transmitted infections, a change of condoms, if moving from anal to vaginal sex, is first step to avoid chlamydia, gonorrhea, hepatitis, HIV, and herpes. The second step is to use water-based lubricants. Oil-based lubricants can damage latex condoms. Some experts don't recommend saliva.

Fecal incontinence is another side effect of anal sex. However, if you take precautions and stop painful intercourse, you should not expect fecal incontinence as a long-term complication.

An ex told me, during our courtship, "Rear is not for

me." My mind went straight to doggy style, but I quickly got back to my senses and realized she meant anal.

I heard the following story:

> We went to the store [and] bought lube and a toy, but we didn't enjoy it. We tried it again, using the techniques we read online, but we still didn't enjoy it. Days later, he told me that anal is not for him. I told him, thank God! I know a lot of girls like it, but it's just not my thing.

If you enjoy it, you have a plus on your sexual repertoire. When performed safely, anal sex is pleasurable and can bring intense orgasms. A 2010 survey found that 94 percent of woman who had anal during their recent sexual act had an orgasm. That's because anal sex allows the G-spot and A-spot to be indirectly stimulated. Besides, the anus is packed with nerve endings. A suggestion: insert slowly, and keep the lube close by. You might need to try it a few times in different circumstances and states of mind to find out if anal is for you.

❑ Combo Sex

Combination sex brings enhancement or surprising results that are more desirable than that of a single element. You can crack two eggs, mix them with bits of cheese or ham, stir the mixture, and there you'll have a delicious omelet. Have bits of bacon, green and red peppers, onion, garlic, and spinach join the mix, and you have a jaw-dropping omelet that's not only more delicious but also richer, healthier, and more nutritional. You may not have it that way all the time, but you should crave it often. The same principle applies to the enrichment of your sexual journey. Making love combined with rough sex comes to mind. You can make your own combinations. Combo is like, "This is it!"

Oral Sex

We humans have been doing many things since the beginning of time, from complaining, betraying, and cheating to putting weed in a vagina. Oral sex happens to be one of the honored ancient traditions. That's right! Research in archaeology and anthropology document ancient lives, including how they romped in jungles and caves.

Depictions of the sexual acts of ancient people, thousands of years ago, have been found around the world. The first traces of fellatio are from ancient Egypt. In the city of Pompeii, Italy—buried by the eruption of Mount Vesuvius in AD 79—archaeologists uncovered ancient baths decorated with erotic watercolor paintings, including depictions of fellatio and cunnilingus. Another ancient building uncovered in Pompeii, a brothel called the Lupanare, includes similar erotic frescoes, as well as signs advertising the services of a prostitute whose specialty was oral sex. The Moche people, who lived on the northern coast of Peru until around AD 560 to 650, made utilitarian ceramics depicting fellatio. The

Kama Sutra, one of the world's most famous erotic texts, was created in northern India, probably in the second century. It includes descriptions of fellatio in various positions.

Even though we turned oral sex—especially cunnilingus—into a sexual delicacy, it's not exclusive to humans. Oral sex has been observed throughout the animal kingdom, from dolphins to primates. Animals perform oral sex by licking, sucking, or nuzzling the genitals of their partners. Several species are documented engaging in both self-fellatio and oral sex. Goats sometimes take their penises into the mouth and produce orgasm. (I have witnessed this in my childhood). In the greater short-nosed fruit bat, the females lick the shaft or the base of the males' penises that are penetrating their vaginas. And so, oral sex is not something for which modern humans can take credit. It wasn't born with the sexual revolution of the 1960s. I believe it was born soon after sexual reproduction, about two billion years ago. It's good that we continue to discover ways to get more of what it's designed to give us, but we dare to claim its originality.

There are many reasons why oral sex is still a slow-moving train of sexual ecstasy. Taboos, ignorance, laws of the land, and churches and other institutions that aim to control societal behavior come to mind. Reports say that any kind of sex in medieval Europe came with lots of rules, which complicated sex even more. Oral sex was on the list of forbidden acts. Penitential literature aimed mostly at monks outlined "correct penance" for a variety of sinful acts. One medieval penitential document from Ireland recommended four years' penance for cunnilingus and five for fellatio (I ask, why mess with women's God-given rights?)

Despite all, oral sex was practiced in medieval Europe. By the nineteenth century, there was a host of English-language slang terms for both fellatio and cunnilingus, including *prick-eating*, *mineting*, and *eating seafood*. The turn of the twentieth century saw a jump in oral sex slang terms, such as *dicky-licker*, *deep-sea diving*, *sneezing in the cabbage*, and the now-familiar *blow job*, arriving in the 1940s. During the twentieth century, the oral sex rate accelerated, possibly as a component of foreplay. By the end of the century, it had become an essential part of the sexual repertoire. Part of this normalization of oral sex was because of the rise of concern for female sexual pleasure and the increased importance placed on the achievement of mutual orgasm. A 1994 study found that about 27 percent of men and 19 percent of women have had oral sex in the past year. The main drive, in oral sex from the twentieth century, was female liberation.

In 2012, a survey from the Centers for Disease Control and Prevention found that among ages twenty to twenty-four, 81 percent of females and 80 percent of males had oral sex.

Despite a dominant cultural view that straight men don't go down on their partners, the numbers say that today's young, straight guys enjoy both giving and receiving. A survey of college students found that 64 percent enjoyed performing oral sex a lot and 24 percent somewhat.

We are still not free of sexual stigmas and taboos, but it seems we can comfortably say that oral sex is something we've been engaging in and enjoying for thousands of years and that we're giving it the service it deserves, especially cunnilingus.

❑ Anilingus

Many men do not practice this sexual act, as they are concerned about stool. First, if a woman is not clean, unless she's drunk, she won't ask for a rim job, nor will she take one. Second, it's just about impossible for your tongue to go deep inside someone's butt and reach any stool residue. If excrement is the only obstacle for you, washing the area with soap and water is sufficient. For deep cleaning, use an enema.

This type of fun cannot be performed abruptly. It requires much more preparation, caution, and foreplay than any other sexual fun. It can be extremely painful, and that kills the purpose. So, once she's aroused, try these moves:

- Kiss and lick her butt cheeks for a moment.
- Circle your index finger gently around her butt hole.
- Lay your flat tongue just below the hole and slowly lap up and down. Avoid her vagina.

- Run the tip of your tongue in circles around the hole. Increase pressure and speed as pleasure builds.
- Use your hands and/or fingers to spread her butt cheeks for room to play.

Sexual stimulation of the anus by the tongue or mouth is another small sexual adventure. It requires support for pleasure to increase and for sustainability, or you will be done in three minutes. Therefore, don't focus on one spot. Use your hands to caress her breasts, or make other movements that enhance pleasure and fun. Use your hands and fingers to tease the vulva, and insert fingers in her vagina to work in synchronization with your tongue and mouth, the main characters. Any other action is a supporting character and must stay at that, or the anal pleasure will be overtaken by the supporting characters.

Doggy style could be a rimming favorite, but missionary is the queen, as it allows for relaxation of both of you, especially when you want to take her to the moon. Yet just like in any type of sex, only both of you can determine what works better and safer.

Dental dams and tongue condoms are useful for safe anilingus. Trimmed nails and clean hands are also recommended. Ensure that once the party is over, you don't bring your tongue anywhere close to her vagina before you oral rinse or brush your teeth. Moving from anilingus to vaginal, whether orally or by penetration, demands washing the hands and penis, rinsing the mouth, and using a condom.

Women should ensure, rather than trust, that their partners use a condom. In either case, immediately after the fun, shower or wash your vulva well with water and soap to minimize the chances of bacteria entering your vagina and do what they do—cause trouble.

❑ **Fellatio**

Fellatio, give head, or blow job, to men, is a sexual act in which someone uses their lips, mouth, tongue, and hands to suck, lick, stroke, and massage a man's genitalia. Its popular name is blow job. It differs from irrumation in that a man is the receiver, not the woman. With that said, don't be shy, women; enjoy it while you give it. Like irrumation, fellatio is the victim of humiliation and degradation without discrimination. I've heard upset women shout, "Suck my dick!" Some guys shout this blasphemy just about every time they're mad or losing an argument with their lovers.

Aside from people's ignorance, this pleasurable sex act is very satisfying and has become increasingly popular. It can give orgasm to a man, and some women enjoy giving head. And contrary to irrumation, there's room to explore a blow job. Supplemental touch is welcomed. Like all other sexual acts, not everybody will respond the same to the same stimuli. There are reasons enough not to scratch this action off the list simply because it seems cheap, poorly satisfying, or unpopular. Are you dumb?

❑ **Cunnilingus**

Let's listen to some stories from John Doe H.

I remember it like yesterday—January 20, 2019. We started with foot massage [and] continued to back massage as part of relaxation, but these actions served as foreplay. I changed to tenderly kissing her legs, inner thigh, then close to her vagina, and I continued with tender bites to her big lips. That move triggered an escalation. In less than a minute, she set the pace. I didn't do much, other than staying the course. I noticed that she was calling for a familiar move, and I immediately responded by putting my left hand under her butt.

Soon after, her butt was up in the air with the support of my hand while I went on with tender bites and gentle licks to her vagina lips. She was side swinging in ecstasy.

My intention was to give her a nice, long head, with enhancement to what we were used to, but I didn't want to break the rhythm. She kept on arching herself higher off the bed. Soon after, she came, and settled back into bed. I wanted to continue, now with my tongue on her clitoris, but she recoiled. Her vagina was extremely wet, and I wanted to keep the heat going while she was rebooting so I started penetrating her. It worked. After a couple of minutes, she was responding with her moves and contractions of her vagina walls, in missionary position. Less than five minutes, we came together. To her, it was coming one more time.

A week later, maybe two, we hit it just about the same, except I didn't have the luxury of penetrating her because she came and crashed instantly. I was so excited about my turn because she was very wet, and I like her like that, but when I looked at her, she was in another dimension already. I realized that it wasn't going to happen. Still tempted, I ran my thumb gently over her vagina lips. She didn't react. I understood that it was not happening to me, so I kissed her, put a blanket over her, sat on the edge of the bed, and for a few seconds, I caressed her hair, and then kissed her forehead, and quietly left.

We had a great setup for sexual adventure: relaxation by watching mimes, stupid stunts on the phone, and listening to comedy on TV. *Impractical Jokers* was our favorite. Then, she would ask me to massage her back or feet, had I not started it. It was always a stress-relief massage, erotic massage, and then eat her out before vaginal penetration and endgame. Going down on her was rarely foreplay. It was rather a full-range action, and she almost always came.

Here we have an example of two sexual encounters where the man goes down on his woman and does a great job. I should rest my case, but I am picky and talkative. For that, I'm going to give you another example before talking about going down on a woman, cunnilingus, giving head, eating vagina, giving her the tongue, or whatever else satisfying a woman by tongue work on her vulva is called.

Somehow, I had a feeling that tonight was going to be special. Maybe because I had finished reading *She Comes First* by Ian Kerner and picked up some interesting sexual moves and was going to use them. As soon as I entered her room, I sensed a good night. She was already relaxed, legs extended and crossed, wearing loose black leggings and a sporty shirt on top her bra.

She was watching funny stuff on her phone. I sat behind her and started to caress her shoulders, like massage. After a minute or so, she was hot, sweating. That made my sexual desire go to the roof. I leaned and kissed the back of her sweaty neck, put my hands under her shirt, and massaged her back. But I was rushing. I slid my hands under her bra to massage her boobs, but I was having a hard time because her bra was tight. I instead caressed them [briefly] over the bra. I took her shirt off and massaged her back, now even more sweaty. I slid my hands under the bra and reached her breasts, but it wasn't comfortable because she was holding her phone. I moved the bra up to get full access. That felt great and increased my boner. I then kneeled in front of her, I uncrossed her legs and started massaging them. I wanted to get her to crazy point quickly, so I bent her left leg to get a better access to her upper inner thighs and to touch her vagina. Soon after, I pulled her pants off. She's now where I wanted her to be, lying on her back, nothing on but a bra and a sexy black crotchless underwear, exposing part of her pubic hair and vagina.

I went on with the erotic massage. She put the phone away and reached for the remote to turn the stereo on.

I was deliberately touching her fat lips with the side of my right hand as I massaged her inner thighs. Many times, she had said, "Don't go there." Not today. My intention was to speed up her arousal and spice things up. It was working! I pushed myself to the edge of the bed to make it easier to kiss her inner thighs. My tender kisses close to her vagina made her shudder a little. That brought glitter to my brain and smile to my heart. I continued, licking her lips over the underwear. This escalated her desire. She lifted her butt to take off her underwear. I finished taking it off. I started licking her left lip gently, probably five licks, and did about the same to the other lip, for three to five minutes. I was avoiding licking her vagina this whole time.

It was magical! Lights out, kids sleeping, neighbors sleeping, and the world was quiet, or we couldn't hear a thing out of the room. The music was helping the fun. I was now enthusiastically licking her vagina from the bottom and up, stopping right before her clitoris, giving it a light lick, and continued to the end of the lips. Sometimes I teased the frenulum. I had my left hand under her butt, and every now and then, I would squeeze the cheeks gently. She was quietly moaning and groaning steadily. I was quietly moaning and groaning but far in between. I inserted my left thumb just a bit in her ass. She squeezed her butt and grabbed it. I continued with my down-up tongue work. After a few minutes I inserted my right index finger into her treasure box. She squeezed her vagina and grabbed it, too. Now, I am in paradise with the brightest smile in my brain and heart. I will tell you why after I finish the story. As I increase the speed and pressure of my mouth on her vagina, she set the rhythm. We were in sync, too. She wasn't coming hard but she had orgasms, and she was very juicy. As we got crazy, I started penetrating her. I gave her a good tongue work and sex to her satisfaction.

OK, I said was in paradise because I had read studies of women's reaction during eating out. Every reaction, such as shuddering when her inner thighs were kissed, the grabbing of the fingers by her butt and vagina, and abundant lubrication, were all the things she did tonight. I also tried the tongue moves and tricks the studies suggested. I was in paradise not only because I was doing it right but also because she matched the women's reaction in the lab study. She's not about talks, hugs, and cuddling after sex and none of that, but I gave her a long kiss. I am sure she got my "You're awesome, baby! You made me proud and respect you more" message.

Let there be no doubts that a sex job well done is intensely rewarding.

❏ Why Youngsters Neglect Cunnilingus and Mature Adults Love It

It's not men's fault (thank God!), nor is it the fault of women's complexity. It's all a product of our biological makeup ingrained in our DNA—divine work. When we're young, we don't take a long time "down there" because penetration is what we have in mind, and we can't wait to start it. That's how we make babies. After age fifty, what we have in mind changes. Sure, smacking it is still there, just not as a priority.

Testosterone is a powerful hormone in both men and women that controls sex drive, regulates sperm production, promotes muscle growth, and increases energy. It decreases gradually as a natural part of aging. In men older than thirty, testosterone levels may decrease 1 percent per year. On top of that, at age fifty (sooner for some and later for others), erectile dysfunction starts its engine. At age sixty, it reaches the cruising altitude to a no-return destination because we should not have kids at that age. Our sperm are not healthy and strong anymore, nor are women's eggs. Don't get me wrong—we can make healthy babies in our fifties, even older, but biology won't smile. A ninety-year-old man might ejaculate but can't impregnate a woman. His sperm count may be low and too weak for the marathon to a woman's egg.

After menopause, women stop producing eggs. Biology is not stupid, like men, to allow a newborn to be nurtured by ninety-year-old parents. Therefore, we don't get it up, and there won't be any parties. No parties, no penetration. No penetration, no pregnancy. Also, stress, frustration, diabetes, the consequences of bad behaviors (such as drugs and drinking), and physical decline, which show their faces after forty, make a man focus on his tongue instead of his penis, proportional to his age.

A young woman tried a man in his eighties out of curiosity. "He didn't get it up, but he sucked me off good," she bragged and then laughed. I am sure he was mad at his penis."

As hard as it is, the older we get, the more frequently our erections hide from us, and when we find them, they slip away fast. If they stay with us, they're weak. The hard-as-a-rock is no more. Such starts its descent after age thirty, and it starts its deadly dive after fifty. Therefore, the younger you are, the more you rely on the penis (penetration), and the older you are, the more you rely on the tongue (licking). Luckily, giving oral is gaining popularity among all age groups. I love it!

Youngsters, forget everything, and indulge in eating her out for real—the best form of satisfying her. Take your time instead of giving it five quick licks and smacking it like a machine—she hates that—or don't go there at all. And when you don't go there, you are pretty much insulting or ignoring her rights. You are a selfish sucker! When she finds out or gets fed up, she'll dump your ass.

By the way, after tricks of biology, the major reason we don't stay long enough "down there" is that we're not sure what we're supposed to do. It's a shame! Let's educate ourselves—read online article and books, and if you can, spare some cash for a sex coach. Learn the basic, popular moves, and give women the sexual satisfaction they deserve, man—not only in cunnilingus but in general sexual activities. You're not a macho man until you master the art of cunnilingus.

Here's a simple technique:

- Whether she's ready for tongue-to-skin action or she has underwear on, don't rush to the promised land. You must greet every member of the royal family before you get to the queen—clitoris.

- Start with gentle kisses to her inner thighs, and walk your way in.
- Give long, soft licks over the underwear (if she's wearing one) until you get the fabric and lips wet.
- Lay your wet, flat tongue at the bottom of her vagina, and lick your way up, as if you're licking a dripping ice cream cone. Give it many, many licks.
- Use the tip of your tongue to make tiny circles over the clitoral hood.
- Use your fingers or hands to gently pull the hood upward to reveal the clitoral head, the glans.
- Start licking with light pressure and speed. Increase gradually as the pleasure builds. (Know that some women's clitorises are too sensitive to touch, even when aroused.)
- When you're into a groove she loves, keep at it until she's over the edge.
- Use your tongue primarily, and assist with your hands, fingers, mouth, teeth, and nose.

The major concern. Aside from an individual connection to sexual myths, taboos, and misconceptions, bad smell is next on the list of major reasons that some men abstain from going down on a woman. This reason is valid. Poor hygiene attracts odors, and odor repels people. Any unpleasant smell kills the mood for sexual activities. In the meantime, believing the misconception that all women smell bad "down there" is a nonsense. The truth is that all women smell different, not just her "down there" but everywhere, as everyone has a distinct smell. Therefore, ensure that what you may label as odor isn't her strong natural scent. If it isn't, then don't perform oral sex to her vulva, even using a dental dam, and wear a protection for intercourse. The odor could be a sign of sexually transmittable infections. Let her know this, as a gentleman.

If you've read my other books, you might've noticed I spend lots of time on chapters, subchapters, and facts I believed we should pay more attention to. Going down on a woman is one of them. The description of the cunnilingus adventures of John Doe described what should be done and what to expect in certain sexual situations. I have done it by the book and got the reaction described in the stories. However, forget about how she reacted. Make sure you know your duty, and perform it to the best of your ability. Unless you're pleasuring a woman with the goal of impregnating her, tongue is the way. In fact, for whatever the sexual purpose is, tongue is the first way most of the time.

17

Wonderland Sex

Wonderland sex is a distinguished and unmatched sexual experience under almost unpredictable conditions. The best state of your mind, body, spirit, and soul, it's full of love, care, laughter, emotion, and—most importantly—playfulness. It's making-love excitement doubled.

Say you have her flat on her back. You kneel over her to look into her eyes and see the beauty of her soul, and she looks in your eyes and sees your unborn children. Your head is clear of prejudice because your heart is filled with love, passion, and desire. There's no moment more important than now; there are no people more important than the two of you right now. You both feel splendid and don't know why. Every look is brilliant, and every touch is wonderfully tantalizing.

You wish him to be inside you forever, and so does he. We are usually swept by this intense love emotion at the highest point of our personalities, which soothes the body, mind, and spirit like no other wonders. We've seen and determined that loneliness is emptiness; splitting up, separation, or divorce is a tragedy; and sexual experience of this nature is beyond pleasurable. With that said, why is this wonderland sex not given to us without hassle and equal to everyone? I don't know the answer. I can speculate that God gave us life, destiny, desire, wisdom, and skills to plan and embark on our journey and enjoy it without reserve. Then, the responsibility lies in us to plan our trips to wonderland sex all the time.

The intricacies of extraordinary sex don't allow for wonderland sex all the time but often. Shooting for wonderland, however, takes us to wonderful places all the time. Wonderland sex is a specialty of the chef. Every day, specialty kills the purpose and becomes regular. Special occasions, such as birthdays, anniversaries, or Valentine's Day, come to mind as dates we should plan to visit wonderland. Save some money, schedule time off, and hire a babysitter so you can spend the time at a hotel, motel, or exotic place. It's a celebration. Have it three times a year, and feel the true joy of the relationship and great sex. Don't indulge in wonderland sex only when it comes unannounced. Bring it to yourself.

18

Frequency

When it comes to how often we party, get down and dirty, nook, or bonk, we are failing miserably. Popular theories say that only moms on welfare and teenagers are getting it a lot. I hope this is not true, but I haven't come across any public documents that discuss the world's population having enough sex, let alone too much of it. Instead, surveys show—not a surprise—that sex frequency is still in decline worldwide. The reason I say it's not a surprise is that a reflection on the ways of modern life tells us that we are unable to have enough sex, let alone a lot of it. I don't understand humans!

Studies from 2009 to 2018 show a decline in sexual activities, including masturbation, anal sex, and penile-vaginal intercourse in different age groups and social status. The report of no sexual activities rose from 28 to 44 percent among young men and from 49 to 74 percent among young women. On the other side of the river, in a study of immunity, people who had sex one to two times a week had more immunoglobulin A (IgA)—the antibody on the front line of defense against viruses and bacteria—in their saliva. People who had sex less than once a week had significantly less IgA, and those who had sex more than three times a week had the same amount of IgA as those who had infrequent sex.

In other studies, men who had more frequent penile-vaginal intercourse had less risk of developing prostate cancer. Men who had four to seven ejaculations a week were 36 percent less likely to get a prostate cancer diagnosis before the age of seventy, compared to men who reported ejaculating fewer times a week. Men who had frequent orgasms (two or more a week) had a 50 percent lower mortality risk than those who had less, confirming the human need for sex on a regular basis. Then, why do we neglect it?

Well, how many times we party under the sheets depends on many factors, including (but not limited to) personality, libido, heredity, finances, and environment. Some people simply do not like to have sex a lot. Others are born with a low libido. A woman may have many lovers and partners, while her sister may become a nun; a man may have ten kids with three women, while his brother has only one child.

I overheard a conversation between two men in their late seventies that went like this:

> "How many kids do you have?"
> "No kids."

"How come?"

"It wasn't for me?"

"Are you married?

"Never married. All my brothers are married, and they have kids. I told them that just wasn't for me."

Naturally, sex frequency is high during the first six months of a relationship and low during retirement. Other factors are in action as well. You could be highly sexual, for example, while your partner is not. You could inherit a low sex drive. You might have a stressful lifestyle, worsened by poverty, and the side effects of technology, politics, and government games might increase your stress levels. Stress is one of the most powerful killers of desire and on the positive effects of sex.

The increase of drug consumption and abuse has made countless individuals have a drastic decline in their libidos. In fact, many people are unable to perform unless under the influence. Instead of using sex for its abundant benefits, they use drugs and alcohol to alleviate stress, frustration, anger, and anxiety and to have sex for fun. Extremely poor communities have the highest drug and alcohol abuse rates. Consistency forms a habit; a habit becomes personal. Habits are very hard to change. Once your sexuality depends on substances, you are on the wrong track, and the younger you are, the worse the consequences.

Human ignorance and stupidity are guilty as charged on the following phenomena:

Culture and traditions. Different cultures and communities have different and varied views of sex.

Religions. Some religions dictate people's social and sexual behavior.

Stupidity. Mistreatment, abuse, nonpayment for services, and murder are some of the reasons that prostitution is banned and outdoor sex is illegal.

Government (racism, discrimination, segregation, and politics). It seems unfair to blame the government for people's poor sexual satisfaction, but it's not. You need to read between the lines to understand this. You could've been born in poverty in a war-torn country. Governments oversee people's social behavior and prosperity. The laws, rules, and regulations for such are beneficial to some but detrimental to most people. Poverty, bias, prejudice, race, discrimination, segregation, and other forms of social injustice cause excessive stress, frustration, depression, anxiety, and anger. Each one alone hinders sex; all combined leave an individual raging—not a good state of mind for sex. These phenomena are human constructs, not God's creation, and the government has its dirty hands on them.

❑ Quantity vs. Quality

"Use it, or lose it"—this is a proven fact. "Wear and tear" does not apply to sex, but quantity is not necessarily a good thing if it lacks quality. The following story illustrates a poor quality of sex.

> I was doing it once on missionary position. I slid my hands under her butt cheeks for deeper penetration. In the process, I scratched her butt. She slapped me hard. I stopped penetrating her immediately. With [anger] running high, I stared at her face as she stared at mine for a second. She said nothing; I said nothing. I thought of pulling out, [leaving], and never [coming] back, but sex is complicated. I have no idea how I stayed hard and continued sex. We both came. I got dressed and left, saying nothing.

They both came, and the incident didn't escalate to drama or tragedy, but that sexual adventure carried anger, which counteracts the benefits. Note that a quantity of poor quality is as close as it can be to no sex. Also, if soon after sex, you engage in a heated argument, the benefits will vanish. You need to guard the benefits. Making love, for example, is high quality. Every time you fall asleep immediately after you've had an orgasm, you've hit high quality. When you have sex primarily to kill frustration or just to please your partner, you've hit poor quality; the benefits won't last.

For most people in relationships, important dates such

as New Year's Day, Valentine's Day, Mother's Day, Father's Day, Thanksgiving, Christmas, each other's birthdays, and anniversaries are sacred party days. Since a day without intimacy is a day when we disobeyed life and cheated ourselves, it's our duty to find ways to serve our sexual desires well and collect the benefits. Therefore, combine your personality with circumstances to determine the frequency of your getting under the sheets, and do your best to fit in the positive quadrant, especially with regard to quality.

❑ Too Much of Good Thing

Too much of good thing is bad for you. If you drink too much water, eat too much food, sleep too much, or stay in the sun too long, you will suffer the consequences. When we talk about too much sex, we are in ambiguity land because there doesn't seem to be such a thing as too much sex. Your vagina can tell you that she's not feeling well, or that you just had a rough ride, or that a session was long and uncomfortable, but she won't tell you that she's had enough. When a woman tells you that her vagina is tired, she means that her energy and desire have left, or she's not in the mood. It's not her vagina's game but a mind trick you should respect because your lover has that right. A sex worker will not call it the day because her vagina demanded it but because she's run out of gas, even if all she does is lie there and wait for the client to finish. Various online information states that

Lisa Sparks, an American porn star, holds the world record for having sex with 919 men in twelve hours on October 16, 2004. I assume that her vagina somehow, at some point, shouted, "Enough!" That was an exception to the rules, but there was indeed too much sex.

With new lovers, for the first three months, we bang it like rabbits. Then passion and desire recede, and physical exhaustion might settle in. Yet we can have sex well above average, especially when our libidos are high. Despite libidos and situations, however, when we sleep late and wake up late, are tired all the time, are late to work and meetings, or lag in the household chores and other obligations because we're having sex a lot, we are victims of too much of it. Also, having too much sex kills the very elements of sexual euphoria, which are desire and feeling horny. That's why three times a week is the average, as it allows us to miss each other and to build sexual need and desire.

Youngsters, please beware of the media, the internet, and hip-hop sexualization that drives you to believe that you must have sex every day, everywhere, in any way. The game is hot, the show is intense, and the minds behind the scenes are powerful hypnotizers. Intentionally or not, they are sowing seeds of sexual failure in you. These will germinate a committed-relationship roller coaster, triggered by too much sex before the fact. Be in charge of your destiny and sexuality through wisdom and enlightenment. Be sure of your needs, and satisfy them within your possibilities. Just dismiss the idea that getting down and dirty all the time equals too much. Instead, remember that what seems to be too much for one person is not so for everyone, and a lot is not necessarily too much. When there's no doubt in your mind that you are having too much sex, slow down before the storm hits.

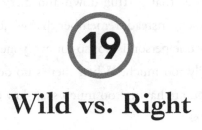

Wild vs. Right

Wild is rough sex that's out of the ordinary. It's fun, interesting, and fulfilling. It's also demanding. Because we age every day and suffer physical and physiological declines as a result, we should take care of our health, nutrition, and fitness to enjoy the wild side to the best of our abilities.

Be wise, and don't believe every story you hear or all the stories your friends tell you. When they say, "Me and my girl, we go wild all the time," or "My wife likes it rough all the time— rough and wild," they may mean intense all the time or, probably, intense sometimes. Remember that people exaggerate to collect credit over their peers. If they go wild a lot, it's because drugs and alcohol are the driving forces, or they don't have sex on a regular basis. Women's sexual desires are regulated by the phases of their cycles. If they are experiencing PMS, they might not want you to get close to them, while during ovulation, they might entice you and never say, "Leave me alone. Don't touch me. My stomach hurts, and I have headache."

From a simplistic viewpoint, there's no right or wrong way to have sex but there are rules for more pleasurable sex, and there are moves that make it dull or even painful. *Right* has a lot to do with the sexual education, culture, tradition, philosophy, psychology, and sexuality of a person. Right is the combination of your experience and what's been proven to work. You can get it right by the application of the algorithm, principles, and obedience to the patterns and protocols. This may sound absurd in sexuality, an extremely subjective subject, but it's not.

No two people experience pleasure in the same way, but some sexual acts bring similar results. Laboratory experiments have shown that some specific tongue moves on a woman's vulva trigger specific responses common to most of the participants. We know that if we prepare our minds before a sexual act, and we have the tranquility of body and mind, we will begin with foreplay and proceed to oral sex, followed by penetration. We've taken the proven steps to the right sexual activity. We won't get the same result all the time but the best that there is. Every time we perform any task with the application of the right procedures, we have reason to feel proud and should accept the outcome with pride.

The first few sexual encounters with a new partner can be a disaster if the right sexual moves are not applied. That's guaranteed to give a bad impression or possibly end the relationship. With practice, we'll discover what works best with our partners, but the basic moves must be applied always.

Treat your lover right, do it with common sense, and use moves you both have found enhancing to your pleasure. Frequently mix wild with the right, and your parties will always be in good hands.

Lights On or Off?

More than once, with different women, I started off on the couch with her. After things spiced up, she took me by the hand and said, "Let's go in the bedroom"—it was a soft demand. More than once, with different women, I've been asked to close the door and shut off the lights. And many times, with different women, we closed the drapes before the action. Does this mean the living room is too open for enjoyable sex and bright must be out? Let's understand it.

Let's leave the great apes alone, as well as our closest cousins—bonobos and chimpanzees, which gave us about 98 percent of their DNA—and refer to our true human ancestors, the Homo sapiens from millions of years ago, who romped in the jungles of Kenya, Africa. Any sexual act had to be performed during sunlight, where it was easier to find a mate and stay vigilant during the action. Night was for resting but primarily for shelter and safety. As Homo sapiens kept evolving, they rapidly left our ancestors behind on the way to becoming the untouchable and much-envied creature in the animal kingdom—the modern humans.

Anthropologists continue bringing to light new discoveries and data that show how close we are to our ancestors, based on the genome, but whatever the real percentage of DNA difference, it gave us the sense of ourselves, the ability to think, and the most important gift of all, which has given us headaches in trying to understand its mystery – the mind – and it made us the one. This explains our unmatched abilities to fall in love, love, care, nurture, and enjoy sex like no other animals. To unwrap our distinguished gifts, we had to replace conformity with free will to fulfill the journey God laid out for us, using our ability to plan, organize, implement, and control our lives. That's why we don't have sex when the environment isn't suitable. We say, "Forget sex out in the cold! What's the heated bedroom for?"

We needed private places to celebrate our unique sexual gifts, so we built huts, caves, and houses, but those weren't satisfactory. We built homes with bedrooms, hotels, and motels. Bedrooms give us the option to have sex either with the lights on, dimmed lights, or lights off.

We can only imagine how much our ancestors would envy us. Nonprime species don't have the brain power to understand, hate, or envy us. We're too far out of their league. And we don't care because we are what we are— God's best creation endowed with powers to grow in all corners of life, especially sexually, and to obey our desires and lust.

From all that, some couples feel more comfortable with lights off; others prefer lights on or either one. Is this just the matter of choice, or are there huge tradeoffs? Probably a little bit of both.

Sex with natural or artificial light has more safety. Regardless of the sexual position, lights allow for the awareness of our surroundings. Even in rear entries, especially doggy style, which is a completely submissive position, the receiver still has safety brought by the lights. Having sex under brightness allows for the lovers to look at each other's bodies for appreciation, to watch their reactions from the pleasure they are receiving, and to see where they're going. All parts of a vulva are easily seen with lights on. That takes away all excuses for, "I am sorry; it slipped into your butt," or makes it that you don't have to say, "Wrong hole." Lovers who are very confident and in love like brightness because their emotions cannot only be felt but also seen.

A sexy, beautiful, and active lover in bed likes lights on for appreciation and showing off. Most guys take lights on any day; we are visual creatures. Some experts say that lights increase testosterone, the man's sex hormone. A friend told me that he likes watching a woman's fat ass bouncing as he smacks her in doggy style. He also made a good point, which is that with lights on, we can see if everything is clean or whether something is off.

As to sex in the dark, the matters are more complex. Shy women and lovers who do not feel comfortable with their bodies—whether because they think they are ugly, fat, or skinny, or their genitals are not appealing—prefer sex in the dark. That is bad and stupid view, but it's their business. Others simply feel more empowered in the dark. Decades ago, a friend said that he does a good job in the dark. It was sufficient for me to understand that he preferred sex in the dark.

Since sex is something extremely private—except on porn—in the bedroom with doors and windows shut, curtains closed, and lights off is the best setting. We evolved to have sex as the last thing before we go to sleep, since the time we lived in caves. We men burn ourselves physically during the day more than women, so we evolved to crash after an orgasm quicker than women. Nothing helps people to recover from physical exhaustion more than sleep. It's true that, many times, we men want to go on after she has had an orgasm, but we retreat because she's already knocked out. Any attempt to wake her up for more action might be an invitation for trouble.

Once the caves became our shelters, sex in the dark and at night became dominant, but here's what makes dark a winner: humans have a higher degree of sexual pleasure. When we close our eyes during sex, we travel into the imaginary world, which reduces distractions and makes us feel the sexual arousal more intensely. That explains why, even when we have sex in the dark, we tend to close our eyes. Our sexual session is, on average, thirty to forty-five minutes or as long as erection and pleasure persist. Even if all happens in five minutes, the dark is a hypnotizing drug, and closing the eyes and traveling with the imagination is a feel-good sensation.

Lights on or off, just have sex as often as you can. Enjoy it safely and without bias.

Fantasyland

The most popular sexual fantasy is having a threesome. Girls prefer to hit it with two guys, and guys prefer two girls. But fantasyland is big and free, with no boundaries, guard dogs or security guards. You can have sex in public, with a stranger, or with someone much older than you. You can be tied up or tie someone up. You can be masturbated by a stranger or friend, be dominated or dominate someone, or watch couples or two women having sex. These are the popular fantasies, but they range from simple, such as romantic sex, to astonishing, such as rape and physical punishment (seriously?). Here are some of them:

- Voyeurism. Arousal caused by watching an off-guard person or people engage in private intimacy or sex.
- Exhibitionism. The act of becoming aroused by others, consensually, who watch you having sex or exposing your body parts. These actions can be

problematic if someone is unable to control their urges, or legal issues arise. In the USA and many other countries, it's illegal to watch or record people having sex without their permission.

- Sex in public or unusual place. This popular fantasy may fall under exhibitionism. In a study, 81 percent of men and 84 percent of women were aroused by a public sex fantasy. Acting on this fantasy is troublesome, as public nudity is illegal in most states, and sex acts in public are illegal in all fifty states. I believe such social laws are applied worldwide.

- Role play. The assumption of another identity. For example, it can help people play out fantasies of a power imbalance, as strangers, or any role whatsoever.

- Cosplay. The act of dressing up like someone or something else (from movies, books, video games). Some people enjoy impersonating a character during sex.

- Multiple partners and group sex.

- Same-sex partner and sex with famous people

- BDSM (bondage, discipline or domination, sadism, and masochism), including much of rough sex. These are considered off-the-chart freaky sexual activities. It can involve a variety of kinky actions and things, such as tying up, spanking, blindfolding.

Some people like to be dominated or are aroused by light restraint; others, by intense physical pain, for example.

When it comes to sexual fantasy, single people and people in open relationships have a better chance than committed or married people. My friend's boyfriend wanted a threesome involving her, but she wasn't sure she could watch another girl sucking her boyfriend. On the other hand, her boyfriend didn't approve of her having a threesome with two guys. Jealousy, competitiveness, and an inferiority complex could be the problems. A lover—man or woman—could interpret the pleasure given by the other partner as better than what he or she ever could give. He or she feels obligated to do better next time with his or her lover. Therefore, you must know and understand what it entails to be in this dangerous sexual zone. When you get it straight, you can have a threesome involving friends or strangers or both. The sky is the limit. Threesome is a strange, powerful thing that can galvanize your relationship but also can ruin it. Don't let it linger forever in your imagination.

Men beat women in fantasies and are more willing to act upon fantasies (hallelujah!), while women are more willing to leave fantasy in the imagination. Yet just because you have fantasies doesn't mean you must or want to act on them. If you do, it is important to keep consent, respect, boundaries, and the laws of the country in mind, and use proper protection. Ensure that fantasies don't become your best friend forever—your partner is and must always be—but keep them in a special place.

Sexual fantasies are a common, normal, and healthy part of sexuality.

22

Orgasm

Orgasm (sexual climax; *orgasmos* from the Greek) is the explosive discharge of a sexual excitement buildup during the sexual response cycle. It's usually associated with involuntary muscle spasms in multiple areas of the body, up to euphoria.

"Why does it feel so good?" one asked.

"It's the biology trick, so we can have sex again, and again, and again to increase chances of pregnancy—procreation!" the other answered.

"Why do women experience it the greatest?"

"Their lives are harder," the other responded.

"I doubt that," another said. "Unlike men, God is just."

❏ Women's Orgasms vs. Men's

The saying is that when God created a man, he looked at him and said, "I can do better than that," and he created a woman—beautiful and special. I believe that. Whether or not you do too, science continues to prove that women are special, and men are not so much. To be fair, men are special. Women are more special. And women's orgasms beat men's by far. Here's why and how women have an incredible journey to orgasm adventures, and men have just a river of joy flowing to a woman's ocean of orgasmic wonders:

About two billion years ago, sexual reproduction began among the species. In humans, this process (along the evolution, I assume) is as follows:

A man and a woman have sexual intercourse when a woman is ovulating. He ejaculates 75–100 million sperm into her vagina—insemination. (Others believe the number can be up to 300 million!) Those sperm travel through the cervix to join an egg in the ampulla of the fallopian tube. Only one of them penetrates the egg. The result of this union is production of a zygote cell, or fertilized egg. This is pregnancy. The zygote cell is pushed to the uterus, where the pregnancy journey begins.

A full-term pregnancy is forty weeks. Although it can vary—thirty-seven to forty-two weeks—it is divided into three trimesters, each lasting between twelve and fourteen weeks (about three months), and each comes with its own specific physical, emotional, and physiological drama. While the first sign of pregnancy can be a missed period, the first trimester is marked by overwhelming changes and transformations in coming weeks, such as:

- Tender, swollen breasts
- Nausea, which often begins a month after pregnancy (with or without vomiting; notoriously called morning sickness, even though it can strike at any time of day or night)
- Increased urination
- Fatigue (your sugar level and blood pressure are lower, and increased hormones, such as progesterone, turn you into a cat)
- Food cravings and aversions (your taste buds change, and you become sensitive to certain odors.)
- Heartburn
- Constipation

During the second trimester, which is the most comfortable period for the majority of pregnant women, the following occurs:

- Expansion of uterus and abdomen
- Dizziness and headaches
- Body aches
- Increased appetite
- Stretch marks on stomach, breast, thighs, or butt
- Change in skin color around nipples
- Itching
- Swelling of the ankles or hands

The third trimester, during which you'll visit your doctor more frequently, brings fewer changes but lots of inconveniences, such as:

- Increased back pain
- Mobility restrictions
- Discomfort sitting down and standing up for a long period
- Travel restrictions

Cruise ships usually don't allow women over twenty-eight weeks pregnant on board, and airlines advise them to get permission from their doctors. On top of all that, you must have more doctor visits to test your urine for protein, check your blood pressure, listen to the fetal heart rate, measure the length of your uterus, and check your hands and legs for swelling. Often, you'll take vitamins supplements, especially iron.

Then, there are the many things that please you, such as drinking, smoking, sports, and kinky and rough sex, from which you must abstain during pregnancy. Pregnancy makes you feel delighted, anxious, very happy, and exhausted, although not all at once. It adds lots of stress to your life, yet the most horrifying experience women go through—labor—is on the way.

While women endure pain and sacrifice for reproduction, men monkey around, and some couldn't care less.

The torturous journey of pregnancy is the main reason

(but not the only reason) that women are gifted with an ocean of orgasmic wonders.

All the way from the jungles of Africa, both men and women went through daily sacrifices, and women got the short end of the stick. Men had superior physical strength to handle the hurdles in jungle. Women stayed home (cave), caring and nurturing kids and were ready to pleasure their men for what they brought home. This developed superior emotion, love, and care. They needed sex after a hard day's work. Just the physiological changes women go through every month is enough to grant them the right to enjoy sex more than men. And so, women have more erogenous zones and a vulva and a long network of pleasure triggers, including the clitoris, and the ability to have multiple orgasms and to orgasm longer and more intensely than men. Women are quicker than men to recover in the refractory period.

Men's sexual network consists of the penis (with only four thousand nerve endings—half of what a clitoris head has), the anus, and other secondary erogenous zones. Men's multiple orgasm is rare and doubtful. The traditional view of male orgasm is that there are two stages: emission following orgasm, almost instantly followed by a refractory period. The refractory period is the recovery phase after orgasm during which it is physiologically impossible for a man to have additional orgasms. Let's be honest: a man's orgasm is nothing more than a reward for helping a woman achieve the height of her pleasure. Guys, let's be compassionate, not angry or jealous!

❏ Types of Orgasms

There are different types of orgasms, from intense vaginal pounding to sleep orgasm. Some are well orchestrated, and others are just a joke.

Here's what science says: multiple nerve pathways is one reason for the variety and complexity of orgasms that humankind experiences. The pelvic nerve transmits sensations from the vagina and cervix, rectum, and bladder, while the vagus nerve communicates signals from the cervix, uterus, and vagina, bypassing the spinal cord. These distinct nerve pathways show the complexity of sexual responses and the reason why we can reach orgasm from stimulation of many body parts.

Feet, for example, are next to the genitals in the brain's sensory map. As a result, the connections between these areas can sometimes get crossed, and the feet become an erogenous zone for some people.

Orgasms arise from stimulation of the genitals, but several factors play a role. The brain, for example, is involved in the entire process. The pituitary gland lights up, and the nucleus accumbens and ventral tegmental areas are activated. The hypothalamus goes into overdrive, and the center of reasoning and behavior shuts down momentarily during sex. Not all of us experience orgasm in the same way.

Some people might get it and not know it, and others do not orgasm at all. Let's start with the unusual.

Erogenous zone orgasms. Some women can orgasm from kisses on the neck or a caress on the inside of their elbows and the back of their knees.

Dry orgasm. This is an orgasm without ejaculation.

Rubbing orgasm. Tribadism orgasm happens when a woman rubs her vulva against her partner's vulva, especially for clitoral stimulation. This may involve vulva-to-vulva contact or rubbing the vulva against the partner's thigh, stomach, buttocks, arm, or other body part. Also, some women have large clitorises and/or big lips and are easily aroused. Wearing jeans, for example, can allow for rubbing of the inseam against their clitoral heads. One of my exes had that ability. Vigorous dances with close body contact and rubbing can lead to rubbing orgasm.

Cervical orgasm. Controversial but real. Once, I asked a friend about the specifics of her orgasm and she said, "OK, contrary to what's called rule, my clitoris is way too sensitive to give me orgasms by stimulation. I enjoy deep penetration. I guess it's called cervical orgasm."

Not every woman can easily get a cervical orgasm. The cervix must be stimulated by a penis or sex toy. Only shallow vaginas make the job easy; the cervix lifts during arousal as part of the process of vaginal extension to accommodate the penis.

Only in a lab and through special procedures with

sophisticated instruments can the cervix be stimulated without vaginal stimulation. The deeper into a vagina, the less sensitivity, and some researchers say the cervix has just a few nerve endings; others say none. Like the G-spot, cervical orgasm can be a product of something else. I do believe, though, that cervix penetration is possible, and it enhances sexual pleasure during vaginal penetration. Otherwise, why do many women love big penises? Whether or not cervical orgasm is a thing, once you enjoy cervical, have fun and be aware of the consequences.

Sleep or unconscious orgasm. Don't we all hate it when our brains act freely and get us in trouble? During childhood, we might have been punished several times a day, as we couldn't stop. And we got punished for peeing on the bed. Then puberty got us in trouble with wet dreams (well, more an embarrassment than punishment.) Brain, why do you do that to us?

An orgasm in our sleep is not welcomed by all. I hated it because it was my brain having fun, not me. I woke up angry every time it happened. Well, too bad; sleep orgasm is real and beneficial.

Spontaneous conscious orgasm. This type of orgasm is like sleep orgasm—an orgasm without sexual stimulation—except it happens when you're wide awake. And it has more consequences. They can come as a short and solitary bliss or a continuous stream of separate orgasms. Some people find them pleasurable. For others, it is disturbing. It can be painful and drastically hinder your ability to sleep well, complete tasks, or enjoy sex.

Researchers have identified some triggering factors, such as persistent genital arousal disorder (PGAD). The clearest symptom is a feeling of sexual arousal without any sexual stimulation. In women, this may cause feelings of arousal in the genital area, including the swelling of the clitoris, vagina, vaginal lips, and nipples. They can last from a few hours to a few days. In men, there is pain in the penis or erections that last for hours. Although having an orgasm brings temporary relief, the overall sensation usually returns shortly after. Certain medications, such as rasagiline, a drug commonly prescribed for Parkinson's disease, or serotonin reuptake inhibitors, which are used to treat depression, cause spontaneous orgasms, but PGAD—the specific cause of which is often hard to identify—is the elephant in the room.

Let's talk about "too much of good thing is bad for you."

Birthgasm. Some people experience orgasm during vaginal birth. It seems women's brains give away spontaneous orgasms to relieve pain and anxiety during labor.

Coregasm. A coregasm is an orgasm that happens while you're working out. It's been recognized since the 1950s and is referred to as exercise-induced orgasm (EIO) or exercise-induced sexual pleasure (EISP). It happens to more women than men. Abdominal exercises, biking, weightlifting, climbing ropes or poles, and captain's chair can give you spontaneous orgasms.

Nipplegasm. Although only about 15 percent of women come by nipple stimulation, nipples have tons of nerve endings. Science has proved that neurons in the genital sensory cortex fire up also when nipples are stimulated. To some people, it can be a sneaky one—toes curling—and to others, pleasure builds up, spreads throughout, and leads to a powerful orgasm. Like the clitoris, nipples are living proof that "great things come in small packages." Explore your nipples as much as you can, and enjoy their orgasms.

Hand-job orgasm. This orgasm is the best when we give it to ourselves, as only we ourselves can feel the true stimulation needs and know best how to feed the needs.

Blow-job orgasm. I believe it is worth noting that not everyone can unload by having his penis sucked. A friend told me that not even sex workers can make him come when they suck him. In one of my short-lived relationship trials, my girl got mad on our first naughty adventure because I enjoyed her blow job but didn't come. Those who come can have fun and intense orgasms.

Anal orgasms. I have heard, "I consider myself a very sexual person. I began masturbating at a young age. Anal sex just works for me. It gives me an intense orgasm sometimes."

Vaginal orgasm. Vaginal as well as anal orgasms are achieved by penetration of the penis, fingers, or sex toys.

o *G-spot orgasm.* This one is brought to you by prolonged stimulation of the G-spot. (Remember that the existence of the G-spot is debatable.)

o *A-spot orgasm.* What is it? Sometimes known as the "anterior fornix erogenous zone," deep inside the vagina, between the cervix and the bladder, about two inches higher than the G-spot lives the A-spot. When stimulated by deep vaginal penetration, it produces pleasure up to orgasm. Joanna Doe says, "I always needed really deep, rough penetration to orgasm. I couldn't understand why. All my friends were getting orgasms with normal sex, even cheap sex, but not me. I know everybody's different, but what the hell? It was only after I read an article online that I understood my A-spot must be stimulated for me to orgasm."

Combo orgasm. To achieve a combo orgasm, you combine clitoral and vaginal stimulation; anal and clitoral stimulation; or vaginal and anal stimulation. Orgasms achieved by multisensory stimulation can be exciting, as pleasure comes from various sources. Most women need vaginal penetration with clitoral stimulation all the time to come. One of my exes once told me that when I didn't put a finger in her butt, she didn't come strong.

Clitoral orgasm. I've saved the best for last because no orgasm encompasses cunnilingus orgasm, simply because cunnilingus is the king of sexual pleasure, as stated by philosophy and proven by science. Neither philosophy nor science cares about your reasons for denial of the fact. Cunnilingus orgasm is brought to you by your partner eating you out. Eating you out encompasses stimulation of your clitoral head. The most common way for a woman to achieve the most powerful and joyful orgasm is by direct and consistent stimulation of the clitoral head, manually, orally, or by other friction against the internal parts of the clitoris. Although indirect clitoral stimulation—via vaginal penetration, for example—can be sufficient, statistics show that 70–80 percent of women require clitoral stimulation to achieve orgasm. Clitoral orgasm is easier to achieve because the head has more than eight thousand sensory nerve endings to provide the utmost sexual pleasure, and it's the main reason women enjoy sex more and have more powerful orgasm than men. (Guys, no need to get upset over this. Women deserve it all, so ... suck it up!)

❑ Vaginal and Clitoral Categories

In 1905, Sigmund Freud, an Austrian neurologist and the founder of psychoanalysis, proclaimed clitoral orgasm as an adolescent phenomenon and that proper sexual excitement of mature women was a changeover to vaginal orgasm without any clitoral stimulation. Freud's theory made penile-vaginal intercourse the key element to women's sexual satisfaction without providing evidence. Because Freud was very influential, many women embraced his penile-vaginal theory and later felt inadequate, as they couldn't achieve orgasm through vaginal sex. (I feel sorry for them and hope they found a way to dismiss Freud's biased proclamation and that they enjoyed sex as it came to them. By the way, Freud admitted the scientific discovery that proved him wrong.)

Fortunately, Alfred Charles Kinsey published the result of his interviews with thousands of women. Most of the women surveyed could not have vaginal orgasms and very few inserted fingers or objects into their vaginas when they masturbated. He "criticized Freud and other theorists for projecting male construct of sexuality onto women" as his research concluded that the clitoris is the main center of sexual response, and that vagina is "relatively unimportant" for sexual satisfaction. He concluded also that satisfaction from penis-vagina penetration is mainly psychological or the result of referred sensation. I believe it is both and more.

Claims that the vagina can produce orgasm is a debatable subject. I would vote favorably because in addition to the vagina's low concentration of nerve endings, the vagina has other functions. Initially, female orgasm was divided into two categories: clitoral orgasm and vaginal orgasm. In 1973, Irving Singer theorized that blended orgasm was the third type. Because he was a philosopher, his suggestion was, much like Freud's, generated from descriptions of orgasm in literature, rather than laboratory studies.

In 1999, Whipple and Komisaruk proposed cervix

stimulation as being able to give a fourth type of orgasm. The problem is that women's orgasms by means other than clitoral or vaginal are less prevalent in scientific literature, and most scientists see no difference between female orgasms. What about anal orgasm? So, what a mess! My two cents' worth is that female orgasms are complex and complicated. Whether or not all orgasms are generated by the clitoris (I believe that!), educate yourself as much as you can, and explore all possibilities.

❑ How Do They Come?

If we go with the movies, songs, and stories of friends, there's only one way to have an orgasm—squealing, screaming, insanity, scratching, biting, crying, and laughing, with earth-shattering and volcanic explosions. The most popular description is "like fireworks." Some women do have orgasms like that—loud and dramatic—but they are the exception.

First, orgasm is the ultimate sexual experience that comes in such ways and styles to the extent that there isn't a universal definition of it. Second, not everyone's reaction to stimuli is aligned with the scientific pleasure algorithm. Third, not everyone is a screamer. Others say talkers and screamers are fakers (I know some people who are real screamers, though), and others may lie in describing their orgasms if they think their orgasms might be too off-the-chart.

I am proud to inform you of what I obtained from porn (some reactions in porn are real), books, sexologists' people's survey, and online materials during the research for this book. To many women, orgasm is a powerful explosion of a feel-good sensation that gradually built up like a wave and spread over their entire bodies. This sensation can last thirty seconds or more. Here are the varieties:

Tiffany said, "Usually, my legs go numb for a couple of seconds. I've had some that made my lower body shake, though. But it's never all over my body."

Joanne said, "It's hard to describe it, you know. Sometimes, it's like a wave of tingling, followed by numbness in my legs; then comes euphoria. Sometimes, it's so strong that tears fill up my eyes, but other times, it's like it's happening but not really. I am a crier. My friends said that I don't orgasm. I 'crygasm.'" She laughed.

Heather said, "My partner was fingering me, and then I started to feel a deep aching in my stomach, and then it was like all my clenched muscles released all at once. That's the only way I can describe it."

Marylou said, "I was so flushed afterward. I didn't know what had happened to me. I was sweaty, and my legs wouldn't stop shaking, even after I came."

Deborah said, "I usually go tingly, my legs go numb, and my face is flushed when I come. Sometimes, I even lose feelings in my hands."

Brenda, the filthy mouth, said,

I had my first orgasm when I was twenty-nine. Don't get me wrong; I've been screwing since I can remember. I had screwed a lot of guys, even some real men, but none of those sucking suckers gave me an orgasm. I don't know if it was me or them, but it never happened. Or it was so light that it did count as a freaking orgasm, now that I know how a real orgasm feels, you know. I never masturbated because I didn't feel the need. Well ... until one day! I got myself a freaking vibrator and had fun with my clit. God, that felt so freaking good! It was like I went to the freaking moon and back. My body was completely exhausted after I came. I was shocked. I remember lying there in disbelief, tears in my eyes ... When my senses came back, I said to myself, "That's how you freaking come." From that moment on, I found myself real, with my freaking moans and groans too, and I wasn't faking shit anymore. Now I come every time, but my orgasms are still the best when I use my freaking vibrator.

❏ Haven't Got It Yet?

A great percentage of women haven't experienced an orgasm, despite being sexually active and having plenty of sex. My stance is that unless you have a condition, once you're having sex on a regular basis, you're having orgasms. It could be that you're not in tune with your body's response to sexual stimuli, or you're not interpreting your sexual feelings correctly.

Dismissing the myth that orgasms must be accompanied by screams and fireworks changes the platform of orgasm. Realize that you're having orgasms, and focus on getting them every time you have sex—that should be your priority. If you're sure you haven't been getting it, chances are the problem lies on your lifestyle. If you bond to taboos, for example, you're restricting yourself from sexual activities that facilitate orgasms. If you don't turn every stone, you might never find the treasures buried inside you. Also, your orgasm demand could be too high, or the sexual skill of your partner is poor. You could need a long foreplay and oral play, followed by intense, prolonged vagina-pounding to orgasm. We guys have the tendency to go down on a woman for a little bit and then start penetration. We're designed to last three to seven minutes, and that is proportional to the intensity of penetration.

Many women suffer from low libido and other health complications that lower their sexual desires and enjoyment. Each could play a major role in *anorgasmia*. The reasons why you haven't got an orgasm yet are numerous. Finding them out is your job. Don't take any breaks until you've got what you need and deserve. Your doctor, for example, can prescribe medication to fix your condition.

Unfortunately, some people can't orgasm at all. People who suffer from clitoris mutilation and health conditions, which can sometimes be genetic, account for the reasons so many people can't reach orgasms. Yet medicine has come a long way and is still progressing. Never let go of hope.

❏ How to Get It

Among all the things that separate us from other animals, what stands out are our superior brain power and sexuality. We bond to a lover for loving, caring, sex, and happiness. We are blessed with the thrills of sex, with orgasm first being the elite of sexual pleasure and then for health benefits. It then becomes our obligation to contribute to the party, without reservations. This is a crucial step to great sex. Today's sex toys satisfy all needs and desires as the best supplemental tools to orgasms when the hands and fingers aren't enough on solo play. Combine what you discovered on solo play with what you receive from your partner. Two plus two is four, and nine plus six is fifteen everywhere in the world and in the entire universe, but a human body reaction is not an exact science. Therefore, keep the definition of orgasm off your mind (when you have an orgasm, you'll know it). Focus on your needs, and communicate them to your partner. You may discover ways to achieve tantalizing climaxes.

Here are some hints, adding your imagination to the game. (Disclaimer: some of the following hints are unlawful, taboo, morally rejected, or forbidden in relationships and can be detrimental to your health. You are the only one responsible for all your actions and every consequence.) Try the following:

- Sex in hotels, motels, casinos, on a cruise, and on an exotic vacation
- Sex during ovulation
- Sex under the influence of alcohol or pills
- Outdoor sex
- Sex in a public bathroom
- Sex with your lover's best friend
- Sex after watching friends or sex next to them
- Threesome involving your best friend and a guy you've been dreaming about
- Novelties
- Adding sex toys to the game
- Masturbation with sex toys that tease your vagina and clitoris simultaneously
- Sex with a foreigner or stranger during an exotic vacation
- Sex with your secret admirer

❑ Who Cares?

Just about everybody cares about an orgasm and wants to have it every time they have sex. Many women get upset when they don't orgasm. Some get angry. And others may take matters into their own hands. Printed works reveal that one of the reasons that Lorena Bobbitt cut off her husband's penis was that he always had an orgasm, and she didn't.

Forty-two-year-old Justin, still a player, attests that orgasm does matter to many. In response to my request for insight for this book, he offered the following: "When I see that they are close to come, I stop. Sometimes I even pull out. But man, some of them get really mad. I did that to one girl; she almost killed me!" He laughed for a second and then said, "She got off the bed and screamed, 'What the fuck, man? I wanted to come. Get the fuck out of my house. Get ... the ... fuck ... out, and never come back!' I tried to start again, but she was really mad. Yeah, they all wanna come all the time."

I believe we all should care about orgasm. Orgasms have many benefits, such as improving our immune and cardiovascular systems; relieving stress, depression, anxiety, and pain; and releasing oxytocin, the love hormone—a chemical responsible for bonding, happiness, and caring for others—as well as releasing melatonin, which make us feel relaxed and sleepy after we come. When women orgasm, the vagina, uterus, and anus (and sometimes other body parts, like hands, feet, and abdomen) contract rapidly (three to fifteen times), and some women ejaculate. Who doesn't want to feel that and cash in on the benefit every time they party? I think the answer is, "Nobody or just a few people."

Not all women who aren't having orgasms should be blamed for not caring or trying. There could be complications out of their control, such as orgasmic dysfunction.

❑ Orgasmic Dysfunction and Symptoms

The main symptom of orgasmic dysfunction is the inability to come. Other symptoms include an unsatisfying way to orgasms and taking longer than normal to reach them, whether during sexual intercourse or masturbation. Here are the four types of orgasmic dysfunction:

General anorgasmia—an inability to achieve orgasm under any circumstances, even when you're highly aroused and sexual stimulation is sufficient

Primary anorgasmia—a condition in which you've never had an orgasm

Secondary anorgasmia—difficulty reaching orgasm, even though you've had one before

Situational anorgasmia—most common type; orgasm only during specific situations, such as oral, vaginal, or anal sex or masturbation

Anorgasmia is frustrating and impacts relationships, but you should feel no stigma or disappointment. Many women deal with orgasmic dysfunction at some point in their lives, and there's cure. Some over-the-counter products and nutritional supplements help and/or fix orgasmic dysfunction. Treatment for anorgasmia depends on the causes of your condition. You might need to treat an underlying medical conditions by switching antidepressants, having increased clitoral stimulation during masturbation and sexual intercourse, or clearing your mind of distractions or pleasure inhibitors during sex. Your physician could fix the problem or send you to specialists, such as counselors and sex therapists. A counselor, for example, helps you and your partner avoid and deal with arguments and learn about each other's sexual needs and desire. He or she guides you in dealing with stressors that might be contributing to your inability to reach orgasms.

Sex therapists might recommend female sex hormones, such as estrogen, estradiol, or progesterone, to help increase sexual desire, as well as female enhancement pills to increase the amount of blood flow to the genitals. Testosterone therapy is another option. The Kegel exercise, although recommended for aged-related sexual malfunction, could help. If there hasn't been a cure for your dysfunction, never lose hope while you look for ways to more joyful and pleasurable sex.

Remember that not everybody experiences sex and orgasm in the same way. Take note that no two sexual experiences, whether with a partner or solo, are the same. Even when the scenario is the same as before, the result will be different. Even if the result seems to be the same, it's not. Only the benefits are similar, depending on your state of mind, spirit, and health. That's why exploring in the moment is key to absolute pleasure. Orgasms can be small, happen just once, or don't happen. And they can be multiple in women. They come from a single play, a specific play, or multiple plays. It's foolish to measure yours against others.

Don't worry that your orgasm is mild instead of volcanic, neighbor-disturbing, or frightening to your kids in the room next to yours. Orgasms vary in intensity, and women vary in the frequency of their orgasms and the amount of stimulation necessary to trigger them. While orgasms originate from the genital area, they are often experienced and felt throughout the body.

As every woman's orgasms are different and highly individualized, sex researchers often refer to this uniqueness as *orgasmic fingerprinting*. Knowing that there are countless ways to orgasm and a variety of types and degrees of orgasms, turn every stone in search of stronger, more pleasurable orgasms.

Sex or Orgasm: Which One Is Better or More Important?

I intended to do a small survey on "Sex or Orgasm: Which One Is Better?" After getting 95 percent of the votes for orgasm, I became intrigued and dissatisfied. I decided to add the second question: *Which one is more important?* That turned the tide. Just about all women gave credit to sex, and many guys gave credit to orgasm. A few friends argued ferociously. I stayed neutral and smiling. I only got two answers of "I am not sure," and three "I don't know" answers from the guys. Women responded quickly and assuredly, while most of the guys hesitated. I realized that the two questions were tricky and opened the doors for argument.

To get unbiased and unanimous answers, we must look into the benefits of sex and orgasm separately. First, let's listen to science with regard to having sex, with and without orgasms. Since a man's sexuality doesn't have much to offer (sorry, guys!), let's look into a woman's sexual response during an act, starting at foreplay. I chose foreplay, which is considered the starting point, but remember that sex starts in our minds and then is directed to our brains for management. Foreplay galvanizes the brain and body toward sexual response, where many chemicals and hormones are released into the bloodstream, causing a woman to become what others call "emotionally stoned." Then the following occurs:

- Her skin becomes sensitive to touch.
- The breasts swell and nipples harden.
- An increase in the flow of blood is directed toward the pelvic area to engorge erectile tissues.
- The round ligament between the uterus and the inner lips involves the process of sexual response.
- The clitoral head emerges from its hood.
- The vulvovaginal glands produce a small amount of thick fluid that acts as lubricant.
- The entrance of the vagina narrows, while its depth widens and increases at least two inches in length.
- The clitoral body stiffens, stretches, and elongates.
- The spongy tissue of the clitoral cluster swells, and its ridge can be easily felt protruding from the vaginal ceiling.
- The clitoral head retracts beneath its hood after getting super-sensitive.

- The body temperature, breathing, blood pressure, and heartbeat increase.
- Muscle tension builds throughout the body.

During this pleasure-building, the following chemicals are released:

Endorphins: This feel-good chemical, which reduces pain better than morphine, is responsible for the pleasurable rush or high.

Prolactin: This hormone promotes physiological responses to reproduction, stress, and emotion.

Endocannabinoids: These neurotransmitters are important to rewarding behaviors, such as exercise, social interaction, and eating. They also help the processes of regulating pain, inflammation, metabolism, cardiovascular function, learning and memory, anxiety, depression, and addiction.

Norepinephrine/noradrenalin: This is a stimulating neurotransmitter that regulates dopamine.

Adrenaline: A fight-or-flight hormone secreted by the adrenal glands when we're stressed or facing stressful conditions, its main purpose is to increase the heart rate and blood and oxygen flow to the brain and muscle. It also helps the body to make sugar quickly and use it as energy. It plays a role in many aspects of metabolism.

All the above hormones and neurotransmitters are responsible for many other functions to keep us alive and sane. Any of those hormones and transmitters are activated during any sexual activity, and when released, this leads to the physiological, intellectual, emotional, psychological, and social benefits in the following:

- Bladder control improvement
- Menstrual and premenstrual cramps relief
- Fertility improvement
- Vaginal lubrication increase
- Protection against endometriosis (the growing of tissue outside uterus)
- Burning calories
- Increasing heart health
- Strengthening muscles
- Reducing risk of heart disease, stroke, and hypertension
- Increasing libido
- Reducing stress and anxiety
- Reducing pain
- Reducing blood pressure
- Improving immune function, mood, focus, and concentration
- Improving self-esteem, sexual function, cognition, sleep, and social bonding

As the party continues, the skin flushes, breathing deepens, the heart rate accelerates, and everything tightens in a final clench. Finally, all the muscle tension that has been building explodes in orgasm—a series of quick, rhythmic contractions. The vagina walls and pelvic floor muscles contract rhythmically in approximately 0.8-second intervals (women tend to experience six to ten contractions, and men four to six, generally).

The uterus contracts from an influx of oxytocin. These contractions produce a wave of pleasure, and with some women, the orgasm is accompanied by the ejaculation of a small amount of clear, alkaline fluid. There's also the release of the following:

Dopamine: Known as happiness hormone, this involves motivation, movement, and reward-seeking.

Oxytocin: This love hormone has a wide range of behavioral and physiological effects—sexual, social, maternal. It also helps support well-being, positive social interaction, growth, and healing.

Prolactin: This is the main hormone responsible for milk production after pregnancy and contributes to the feeling of happiness we get after orgasms.

Serotonin: This neurotransmitter helps mediate optimism, satisfaction, mood, reward, among other functions.

A sex act without orgasm gives out all the above descriptions except those of orgasm. The majority of chemicals released during sex happens before orgasm. My understanding is that the chemicals released during or after an orgasm are the surge of what was building from sexual stimulation to orgasm. And God, Jesus, Lord, they do crazy wonders to you during the few seconds they last. Hallelujah! And the effects can last for days. Thus, the verdict goes to sex! And here are the nails to the coffin:

o   Not everyone can orgasm, but everybody enjoys sex.

o   Orgasm can't come without sex.

o   For orgasms to come, we must enjoy sex. When doctors recommend that patients have sex for health benefits, they don't say, "Make sure you come." I am sure they hope you do, but if orgasm is the medicine you need, they would recommend masturbation as first aid.

o   Most of the benefits of sex, with or without orgasm, happen during the journey leading to orgasm.

o   Orgasm is whipped cream that tops the cake. If you only ate the cake, you'd already get all the nutrients. The cake is good, but the topping is delicious. And that might be why people accept the idea that orgasm is more important than sex, to the point of faking it for the sexual satisfaction of a partner or to end the party.

o   Orgasm is the small, silver, second-place trophy, crafted so beautifully, but everybody wants it next to their big golden trophy of sex—the big golden trophy shines brighter next to the small silver one.

o   When you tour the palace, you'd be glad to see the queen, but if you don't, you'll still return home happy.

o   Sex is a need; orgasm is a want or desire. With that said, once you care for your needs, your wants and desires will care for themselves, for the most part and almost always.

I am sure everybody wants the body convulsion and the powerful wave of extreme pleasure from head to toe, over and over again. A friend had it so powerfully that his legs were shaking like crazy. Orgasm is a very special want, as close as it can be to a need. It's greatest contribution to our well-being is better sleep. A better sleep contributes to the following:

• A stronger immune system
• A longer lifespan
• A well-rested feeling
• More energy and enthusiasm

Orgasm is very important to our overall health and well-being. It's just that sex is more important. Sex takes us around the world, and orgasm takes us to the moon and beyond, but we live on planet earth.

❑ The Partners in Crime

God and biology created sex as very pleasurable—a trick so that we can do it again and again to impregnate or be impregnated. But there's more to the pie. If a man impregnates a woman, and he disappears, she's got no chance to raise a family with him. That's where orgasms come in, with loads of oxytocin and other good stuff to make both the woman and man bond to each other. This fact is sufficient to charge sex and orgasm with a partnership in crime—one kills, and the other buries. But the story doesn't end here. Who digs the graves? Jealousy does.

Before we have sex with someone to whom we're sexually attracted, we're jealous because we're afraid of someone else taking away our opportunity to have sex with him or her. After we have sex, we're more jealous because we're afraid of losing him or her. And each time we smack it, we fall deeper in love and become more jealous. We begin thinking seriously about raising a family with him or her, especially when there's a strong chemistry, to secure the treasure in our possession.

Is there a guard? Yes. It's biology!

When women invoke "mom brain," they're typically describing the experience of feeling scattered, distracted, forgetful, or disorganized because of being pregnant or giving birth. A study found a decrease in gray matter—the neurons that form the cerebral cortex and are responsible for social cognition, among other functions—in moms' brains two years after childbirth. First-time fathers experience an increase in prolactin, oxytocin, and estradiol and a drop in cortisol and testosterone levels; they become loving, caring, and less aggressive because of changes in the cortex of their brains. When such phenomena don't happen, some moms and dads could suffer the consequences.

Alfred married his high school sweetheart. Their life after marriage was wonderful, and their sex life was blessed with quantity and quality on the wild side, as both were young with high sexual desire—an incredibly rare match. After five years of celebrating lust and happiness, they became parents. His lifestyle didn't change. He was proud of being a father, but he wasn't much of a dad, still hanging out with his friends as much as before the child's birth. "I simply didn't feel the change. I heard about it, but it did not hit me. I loved my son, and I was happy with my wife. I just didn't change. I regret that it cost me a divorce, but there was nothing I could do about it."

You see, when motherhood or fatherhood hits, your personality upgrades to more loving, caring, and responsible. This upgrade is a positive contribution to relationships, which, in turn, increases chances for more fun under the sheets. More fun under the sheets equals more happiness. Happier relationships last longer and forever.

You'd better believe that sexuality is not a work of chance; rather, it's a deliberate work of infinite intelligence. Either way, it has been a long trip to the understanding of human sexuality, and the progress has been astounding. Yet what's to be discovered is surely mind-boggling. To my understanding, there isn't any bigger mystery than the mind and sexuality. The mind is extraordinarily powerful and complex. Sex is extraordinarily powerful, complex, and incomprehensibly pleasurable. I'm perplexed why sex—something of such a great magnitude of power and pleasure carries a second character within—diseases.

❑ What the Hell?

There is no doubt that sex is one of the most powerful acts, giving us the ultimate pleasure and the dominant way of reproduction. This makes it hard to understand how it can harbor transmissible infections and diseases. "What the hell?" is a reasonable complaint, but I found the answer to my perplexity. It lies in life's makeup.

Every activity triggers a reaction, a desired or unpleasant consequence. What gives us the greatest amount of pleasure has the potential to sicken or kill us. Sugary foods and drinks, for example, are delicious but can give us diabetes, one of the most distressful diseases. Sodium is tasty but can give us high blood pressure, a factor in cardiovascular diseases. Wealthy stars and superstars avoid extortion, kidnapping, and robbery by hiring bodyguards. Having unprotected sex with someone you don't know well is a mistake, and it's stupidity if you picked up him or her on the street. If you let the high and drunk open the doors for "everything goes—and unprotected" you're more likely to host an STI.

The consequences of human behavior are proportional to the quantity and danger of the activities. The consequence of living is death. It's understandable, then, that we get STIs. You can abstain from sexual activity to be 100 percent safe (please don't do that), but you'd rather practice safe sex and have the benefits. It's true that we can only do our best to dodge infections. An old friend, who is happily married, said, "I am always getting an infection. I don't know how people out there do it." Her message was that even when you are safe, you can still get hit, let alone when you neglect. Another friend told me, "Even new underwear gives me an infection sometimes."

But sex is too important to be buried. If you get an infection, see a doctor when over-the-counter medication can't restore your health.

When we understand life's phenomena, "what the hell?" is not a fair question. Just don't be stupid. A close friend died of AIDS at forty-five years of age because he believed it was all government's game and not real.

Never forget that we have the obligation to honor sex without reserve. We are the chosen ones; otherwise, we wouldn't enjoy it more than other animals, and unlike other animals, we have sex in so many positions. Anyone who is not having sex is not only depriving himself or herself of the greatest pleasure but also is missing the healthy sexual benefits. Please, don't do that!

(24)

Positions

We may claim with confidence that doggy style is prevalent in the animal kingdom, as just a few other species, such as gorillas and bonobos, are known to have sex in the missionary position. We humans, the legendary creatures, inherited doggy and missionary positions and then asked imagination to give us more. And we got them, many interesting and some crazy. Well, we are the chosen ones for a reason.

To have a variety of positions up our sleeves is to have another strong pillar of relationship and sexual thrills, next to love, romance, and money, to ensure the fun "until death do us part." Position combinations, for example, are the most powerful bodyguards of long-lasting sexual thrills and the frontline soldiers in the battlefield of sexual boredom. Sadly, we do a bad job with position combinations because sexual pleasure is very tricky, and humans are crazy, to say the least.

First, we are too consumed by smacking it hard and fast and then see you later because we have things to do, especially when our lives are in the fast lane, such as in rich countries where the world is awake twenty-four/seven. Not even retired people have time to relax and have sex without rushing on their minds. This is bad. And we don't seem to find ways to fix it.

Second, the trap of arousal gets us all the time. Arousal is a biological phenomenon designed to elevate pleasure gradually to orgasm, climax, the explosion of sexual tension built during the fun. We can slow it down or even start again from ground zero, but foreplay can escalate arousal quickly, and penetration becomes urgent. The good is so good in missionary, for example, that we want to keep things uninterrupted. And since we rush in everything, we are glad the end is approaching so we can have spare time to catch up on Facebook, Instagram, Snapchat, dating sites, or whatever else we are addicted to online. We can even be desperately focused on getting on with it and getting more sleep tonight. Victimized by the rush and trap of arousal, very often we don't use any of the position combinations in our minds. This road leads to conformity—happy with one or two easy positions or satisfied with less and poor. This is very bad. Tell your lover of positions in your mind for tonight, ask him or her for enhancement, and commit yourselves to make it happen.

❑ **The Practice**

Make a list of sexual positions from books, magazines, or online material. Choose specific days for the trials of a few positions on your phone or printouts—don't try them out in your mind. Keep them visible as you try. Not all positions are possible, even with the assistance of sex furniture. When the height difference is great, lots of positions are uncomfortable, unpleasurable, or impossible. Don't worry about them. Even those positions you can easily do might not bring enough pleasure to make the cut. Your weight and fat distribution may pose a threat to the success of some positions. Fortunately, you can fix this with diet and exercise, stretching, yoga, and so on, proportional to your commitment (I recommend serious commitment because sexual pleasure is the ultimate treasure of life), but many positions may not be worth the hassle.

Whatever you can practice, practice for comfort, rather than pleasure. Once you have dominated a position, pleasure will easily come the next time. This way, you can start another position sooner. If practice becomes a real deal, enjoy the ride today, and get back to practice another day.

For many reasons, including the ability to easily see what you're doing, daytime is the best for practicing positions, but you have freedom of choice.

❏ Position Mastery

During the first three years of marriage, your sexual acts should be about finding what pleasures you both the most, and the years to follow are for fun without hassle. The positions you've tried before must be mastered now. Some of them are more than just a variety. They deserve the honor of distinction. The missionary is intimacy, bondage, communication of the hearts and souls, love, and appreciation. The doggy is vulnerability, surrendering of oneself, and the most trustworthy. Worship them for ultimate pleasure and satisfaction in bed. Get comfortable, and without reserve or prejudice, explore the pleasure of a position. Don't be too quick to abandon a position simply because you had discomfort or little or no pleasure during the first trial.

❏ Above and Beyond Personality Traits

Everyone has a favorite position. Whether popular, such as doggy, missionary, spooning, or cowgirl, all positions come with specific requirements that may override our personality traits, but any sexual act is like being on a team. All players must give all they've got for the success of the game. With that said, you should never feel forced to do something or act in ways with which you are not comfortable in bed but are willing to cooperate for the increase of mutual pleasure or that of your partner.

A missionary position and all its varieties allow your lover to smack you hard and fast without concerns of your being tired, but it also requires that you look at each other's faces, kiss, embrace, caress, and grab with your arms and legs—these actions show best the intimacy, love, care, and pleasure of two bodies, one soul. And the more intense the party becomes, the more vigorous the participation of the partner on the bottom must be to boost the giver's pleasure and enthusiasm.

A cowgirl, which allows for the control of deepness of penetration, tempo, and rhythm, is a variety of missionary that gives you, the receiver, an edge, but it requires your dominant physical participation for a great play. While you ride his penis at your will, use your hands freely, even to stop him from using his hands without your permission. This is your time to shine! Silently (or not) ask him, "Who's the man now? Who's your daddy?"

It came to my mind that doggy, the animal position, is interesting. Contrary to the missionary position, which is a highly visual communication, doggy style is a slutty position. When sexual reproduction arrived two billion years ago, there wasn't such a thing as love, care, passion, romance, jealousy, and so on. Sex must've been like a buffet. The male came along and penetrated the female's vagina and hoped that she would get pregnant and deliver his offspring. And she neither cared nor wanted to know who he was. She needed much sexual intercourse to get pregnant. Why should she care who the father is? But as evolution went on, relationship and family came into the game, with love, care, passion, and jealousy. Both the male and female (particularly the male) wanted to ensure they were raising their own offspring. Then, the missionary position became the second favorite position and the dominant one in relationships. To this day, women who are shy or less romantic favor doggy style.

On the other hand, doggy is a submissive position where the woman deposits all her trust in you. It is comfortable and allows for deeper penetration, among other benefits. And ever since, women instinctively despise sexual approach from strangers and are ready to attack any stranger who dares to approach them with any sexual moves because they need to see the person. Even friends will get that reaction. I believe doggy is everybody's favorite. If you're an exception, I suggest that you reconsider.

Any sexual act involving penetration is an intensive exercise between two or more partners. It is understandable that women are receivers by nature. Also, their higher level of sexual enjoyment requires more concentration, which, in turn, reduces desire for physical movement, which makes many women less participatory in bed and often not leading the game. Fight it. Intense participation will lead to greater sexual satisfaction for both. We men like active women in bed. In fact, contrary to what many women think, men like women who are in charge. It makes the party more interesting, as both of you are working at it. By the way, never shun your desires in bed, as long as those desires are not out of line. Your partner might enjoy your impulse.

Some positions do not allow for mutual participation, thus falling into the exceptions to the rule. Aside from that, you have no excuse for being passive in bed. A considerable number of lovers don't go beyond their personalities to please their partners in bed because, they say, "That is not me." Leave your comfort zone to experiment with new things before you cross them off, or you'll never discover the full potential of your sexual soul. Obey the laws of pleasure, or your sexual adventure will always be below its full potential, which will erode the pillars of your relationship instead of galvanizing it.

Since not every sexual position is doable or pleasurable to every couple, "monkey see, monkey do" is restricted here. So, try monkey see, monkey do what monkey can do. When a monkey puts his or her body, mind, spirit, and soul into every sexual activity, there's a lot a monkey can do to keep the bedroom hot and beautiful. The flames of love, passion, and desire will never die.

25

Good in Bed

Ambiguous expressions such as "great" and "good in bed" spin our heads because we know that being as cold as ice in bed is not ideal, but passive shouldn't be condemned. Active participation is a positive contribution that all men want from every woman, but numerous women like to enjoy the party passively. The sexual party has many splendid guests, and it's almost impossible for magic to make a scene, but there are, indeed, right and wrong attitudes to enhance or kill sexual excitement, aside from your sexuality. And our philosophies of life are powerful agents in making us either great or poor in bed. Here are some of the requirements for great sex:

- Be physically and mentally fit.
- Master sexual positions.
- Be sexually well educated.
- Dismiss social misconceptions and taboos.
- Obey your sexuality, and improve it, if needed.

- Be there, be there, be there enthusiastically.
- Be confident, nonjudgmental, and cooperative.
- Give without hope of receiving.
- Enjoy what you receive.
- Don't rush the process or skip important steps.
- Venerate kissing and cunnilingus.
- Have sex regularly.
- Avoid enhancements unless you must use them for health purposes.
- Learn as much as you can about women's anatomy, characteristics, and sexuality.
- Respect the personality.
- Love her and show her how in bed.
- Put her desires and satisfaction before yours.
- Be with your partner, not with others in your mind, or master the fantasies.

The chances are that anyone lacking most of the above characteristics is fair, poor, or bad in bed. An upgrade is desired but not necessary. The judgment falls in your lap. The practice of some of the above items may not be aligned with your philosophical principles. Apply what falls within your acceptance, and fill in the blanks to your satisfaction.

The complexity and singularity of human beings throw bricks at many aspects of life, including sexuality, and culture, tradition, myths, misconceptions, and other social constructs add salt to the wounds. For example, certain sexual moves do not generate equal power to all individuals. Science brings about the algorithms, and religions and governments forbid their application. I am sure that once you live by scientific discoveries combined with your sexuality and philosophical principles, you will be fit and will deliver what's expected in bed. I guess that makes you good in bed. It should!

26

Relationships

Once upon a time (even though it seems like yesterday), the 1960s woke up, inspired by dreams full of wonder. This decade put on its best makeup, best outfit, and best high heels for a lifetime journey. Confident that, from now on, life would spring instead of slowly walk, the '60s were as ready as they could be. The revolution in all corners of life is what the '60s had up its sleeve. And then it was showtime!

Nations began to ferociously fight for independence. Science and technology took Yuri Gagarin, the Soviet cosmonaut, to space and Neil Armstrong, the American astronaut, to the moon. Manufacturing and industry stepped on the gas. More important, the computer revolution started its Ferrari engine. And if the revolution was to reach to every corner of life, then relationships also got the touch.

I think relationships got a significant piece of the pie. Their wagon came to spike infidelity, skyrocket the divorce rate, and redefine marriage, household responsibilities, and freedom of sex and expression. Older generations claimed that the devil had spilled his evil throughout the entire world and that relationships were a plague. I don't think things were that bad, but drastic changes were in the air. It seems, though, that only now are we recognizing the arrival of the 1960s revolution, as the current chaotic world and living conditions are incomprehensible. And this reality makes the matter of relationships a living nightmare, especially when we find ourselves in search of a soul mate.

❑ Your Partner for Life

When we're young, we don't fully understand the meaning of a relationship. As we grow older and learn the dynamics and meaning of life, we realize that, at some point, we'll have a relationship and a family of our own. Then puberty arrives to close our case; we start falling in love, looking for love, and dreaming of relationships. In societies where we have total control of who we will marry, we plan, seek, and select.

Your partner for life comes with strong strings attached, followed by the strings of his or her family. Strumming or playing those chords can bring horrendous pain to the fingers and arm, and the sounds could be unpleasant to the ear. To avoid that, you need to pick and choose your partner for life without rushing. Even when your partner for life meets all your requirements, you'll face rough waters with deadly waves, particularly if you let the idiocy of your heart pick one for you. And once you start searching, you'll need to ensure that all stones have been turned, including personality, heredity, communication skills, and conflict resolution, among other things, before you make your final decision.

Even though there are enough fish in the water, all beautiful and delicious, none is going to jump out and land in your lap. If you want beautiful and delicious, you might try to be beautiful and delicious yourself. Part of being beautiful and delicious includes education, employment, and finances, the strongest weapons you can have for your success in general and for your relationship. Once you have a higher education, good employment is headed your way. With that, you're on the road to dominating the tricks of finances and to being in control of your destiny. For that reason, consider education, employment, and finances as the three most important keys to the castle of your relationship. When you get this trio under control, it's a certainty that the most beautiful and delicious will come to nest with you and, with a little bit of luck, kiss you from head to toe. Doing it right could be a lengthy and frustrating process, but it's a very wise move that will save you lots of headaches and sleepless nights.

Remember that to build a castle strong from the foundation is to avoid rebuilding it. The material and builders determine a long-lasting castle or a castle that's in decline from day one. If the materials are cheap and the builders unqualified, there will be nasty surprises. A mistake in selecting your partner for life can ruin the branches of your family tree and bring termites to the trunk. It is your obligation to make each new branch stronger, more desirable, and more beautiful. And so, bring the best and be with the best, not the rest.

Dance around to learn the ropes until you are thirty years old or until you're sure that you're fit for a relationship. Then, think seriously about blending two bodies into one soul for life. The number-one reason you should take your time is that rushing can cause you to take whoever comes your way. Big mistake!

❑ The Families and You

Your cousins, nephews and nieces, uncles and aunts, brothers and sisters, and mom and dad will be happy to watch you cherish your pie, hoping that you will share. On the other side, your in-laws have high expectations of you, even if you don't clearly see it. Of course, their main expectation is that you will treat their daughter or son (your lover or spouse) to the best of your ability in peace, love, harmony, prosperity, and happiness, but they also expect that you will add their well-being to your wagon too. You must accept that responsibility and try to please both families while you focus on your own family needs. Take them aboard, but don't get a flat tire.

Also, while you ride along with them, you need to make sure that you are in the driver's seat at all times; otherwise, your wagon could end up in a bad crash. Some in-laws can be a better driver than you. To those, you should offer your seat, watch how they maneuver, and learn their skill so you can improve and take over. You also will need to find ways to deal with suckers in both families. Regardless of how much you do, your sister might never stop complaining that you don't help enough. And a brother or sister-in-law could suck you dry and ask for more.

You can adopt many strategies and take measures while you endure the burden of both families. Part of the strategies and measures include respect for family values, not neglecting your responsibilities, taking advice from those who know better, and remembering that only you can find the magic bullets.

❑ A Family of Your Own

A family of your own is your best treasure. It deserves the best care and protection. If you don't have one, you should find one. Think of this: your kids are the only ones who can ensure the continuity of your branch of the family tree. You must give them the necessary tools to do the job. You could be short of your parents' (and everyone's) expectations but not to your own family. This implies a clear understanding of the total control of your destiny. If your own family is blended with your family, and you are constantly running to your parents and siblings for advice and financial rescue, you'd better prepare for the eternal burning of your ears—a sign that people are gossiping about you.

Since it is almost impossible not to have your family meddling in your affairs, reduce the effect of this bad behavior by keeping your independence, and stand strong and far from threats. Of course, you should keep in close contact and have a strong connection with your family while you build your own, but you are now a branch that must grow on its own, with the obligation of making the tree stronger and better. If the branches are healthy with vivid green leaves, the trunk and roots also are healthy.

You are now split in three: one part to your family, another part to your in-laws, and the third part to the family of your own. You must attend to all three but with a priority to the family of your own.

Raising a family has become a challenge that requires physical, spiritual, and intellectual strength. The social environment—the poison of the internet and social media—makes it almost impossible for you to raise your family by your absolute terms. Emotional distress constantly comes from every direction to rock a family's boat. Single parenting, poverty, unemployment, and underemployment have caused stress and frustration to strike families without mercy.

The head of the household is very tempted to rely heavily on alcohol (a slow death) as a medicine for stress and frustration relief. Chances are the children will be malnourished and have poor home education. Both boys and girls will hit the streets (a suicidal move) to relieve their own frustration, and their being runaways is within arm's reach.

As the train of chaos keeps rolling faster and faster, it will reach the split-up station. And there, the hell can get even hotter. A single mom or dad is left puzzled over the parenting and employment balance. If grandparents can offer some assistance, there will be some relief, but in general, dropping children at a daycare and returning after work to pick them up has proven to be the norm and an impossible task to balance. One child poses a daunting struggle. Double the number of kids triples the amount of struggle. What about the money for childcare?

Single parents (as well as most of the population) earn barely enough to cover the basic needs with sacrifices already. The absent parent (generally the father) must chip in for child support and education. When the courts must step in to enforce child support, more often than not the relationship with the ex-spouse is sour and on old, rusty tracks. It is stress, frustration, and desperation, twenty-four/seven, to the detrimental development of the children. A broken family is a nest for a broken man. A broken man is a man whose power of integrity and strength of character have been lost or stripped away. A broken man might never find his way back.

We have been forced to embrace a relationship that is

severely attacked by the struggles of raising a family, while it also faces a high probability of going through the single-parent phenomenon, leading to broken men and women. And the children are likely to follow in the parents' footsteps.

The main goal of any family is about the same as everybody else's: happiness, prosperity, and empowerment for children. In order for that to happen, children need the tools. The greatest tool happens to be education. Regardless of how well or poorly educated you are, don't mess with the education of your kids. Without it, their chances of success are slimmer, and the odds of their becoming isolated, broken adults are greater.

Part of this game includes your connection to your children's school and teachers. Never miss a teacher-parent conference; ask questions and seek advice. Talk to your kids about the importance of education, and make it clear that you are there to help. Be engaged. If it becomes necessary, and you have the means, find tutors. In fact, once you've determined that the education of your kids is the priority of all your priorities, help will come from all corners. Also, don't allow life and the relationship revolution to laugh at the family you're raising. Don't wait forever to think about it, and don't wait an eternity before you start taking action.

At eighteen, you're in the swinging zone. At twenty-five, you are definitely in the zone of seriousness. Prepare to seriously go to action. At thirty, you are most definitely on the battlefield. In case you are backing down, remember that from a family you came, to a family you belong, and from a family of your own you will leave, or you didn't make the cut. Don't linger in your parents' basement for an eternity—that's a hideout for losers. The longer you stay there, the more comfortable you'll be, and the harder it will become for you to face the outside. Roll up your sleeves and go to work, aware of the tricks of your heart, and be prepared to take the necessary measures. A relationship is serious business. Raising a family of your own could be jeopardized by the tricks of your heart. Don't be a fool. Don't be a loser. Make it count.

❏ Sending Your Sweetheart to Hell

History has shown that many things don't get better with time or maturity. The relationship is one of them. The world, our friends, and our parents constantly remind us of relationship hardships. We are not alone, and relationship hardships are not a phenomenon of the current era. It is part of who we are and the dumb things we do. And it is so because the affairs of the heart are rooted in soft ground. We adults—losers and heroes—have much to say about them. Chances are that you, the youngsters, have experienced love deception and hardship more than once or twice. We all have fallen into the wrong arms, gone to bed with bad partners, received hugs and kisses of death, or have woken up with a nightmare in our laps. And before we recovered, there we were, falling in love again.

The heart, which holds the very key to our emotions and survival, never misses an opportunity to do something astonishingly stupid, such as falling madly in love with the dumbest girl at the mall or the most punk guy on the streets. No matter how smart we are, we're going to be tricked by the heart's idiocy and then stumble, fall, get up, dust ourselves off, and move on, with a lesson learned. But this is not too smart. We could stumble and fall so hard that we pass out or die. We must find a better way, especially when we realize that nothing has more power than our own hearts to put our dreams' lights out or to turn us from a hero into a zero.

Kelsey was a distinguished student from kindergarten through high school. Her good grades earned her a full scholarship to college, and after graduating, she enrolled in law school, mastering in criminal justice. All went very well during the first semester. After that, trouble started to sneak in. She needed a better part-time job to cover her car payment, insurance premium, school materials, food and clothing, and smartphone, as well as helping with her mom's rent. To make matters worse, her junior-high sweetheart, who'd been in and out of jail, needed serious cash for bail. There was no way she could find that kind of money, but she wasn't about to let her sweetheart suffer in prison. She found another part-time job.

Struggling with two jobs, school, and prison visits proved to be too much hassle, stress, and frustration to handle. Some of her responsibilities had to go. She quit school to work as hard as she could to support the boyfriend in prison. She soon realized that she'd bitten off more than she could chew. She was going to die from exhaustion, stress, frustration, and lack of sleep unless she dropped more responsibilities, which she did. She quit the part-time job she had held since junior high. With that came the loss of an income. Consequently, she couldn't support her sweetheart in prison as she had been doing. Going back to school was out of the question.

About a year later, she moved in with the boyfriend. Within a year, she delivered his daughter, her first baby, at the age of twenty. And a year later, she became a single mother.

She'd had many calls to send her sweetheart to hell, but she ignored them. Destiny answered for her, although not without regrets that included her education, which has stayed stagnant to this day.

When we're young, we make all kinds of mistakes and do dumb things with complete disregard to the consequences. It's all good because we learn from our mistakes and have enough time to compensate, except the world has become an increasingly crazier place. Any setback that touches our lives pushes us far behind the game. When you are victimized and badly scarred by your sweetheart, your chances of success in life are severely minimized. Actually, depending on the nature and intensity of the attack and disillusionment, you could be on the brink of taking your life or facing criminal charges, triggered by your sweetheart. To avoid the drama, you must send your sweetheart to hell and take charge of your emotions before the storm. This approach is a mandate after you've been tricked seriously more than once or twice.

Now, hold your horses! Understand where you stand and where you want to go before you start galloping into the unknown and end up in a more horrendous abyss than the one you're trying to walk away from. Don't think that once you send your sweetheart to hell that you're protected from the whips of relationships. You can't be heartless, nor should you allow your sweetheart to destroy your life. You sent your sweetheart to hell so you can prepare to conquer the love you deserve, not the first phantom who shows up in front of you. Kelsey did the opposite. Her new sweetheart wasn't much better than the one she left in prison. As a result, darker times struck her unmercifully.

❑ Who Do You Welcome into Your Heart?

Aiming high and sticking to your dreams helps you steer your life away from tricky, troublesome love roads. But to understand who you should welcome into your heart, you need to become a bodyguard. That doesn't mean you should carry guns and have gigantic biceps; rather, you should learn scanning skills to stay vigilant to the tricks of the heart and be aware of people's hidden intentions. You must train yourself to see, smell, and feel them before anybody else. And you must be prepared because you'll be hit. When it happens, you'll be screwed, thrown off the wagon, and left for dead, except you aren't. You'll endure the consequences of a bad experience before you get up and continue your journey, with one more lesson in your backpack. To be aware of this reality is to empower yourself by deciding who you should welcome into your heart and by preparing for not being blown away by nasty surprises.

No girl dreams of a lazy bum as her adored one. All girls dream of being princesses. No lazy bum is going to give even an inch of that. Boys, on the other hand, want beautiful, sexy girls with nice, firm butts and big boobs—or, a choice of one of my sons, "Girls who won't make me mad when I look at them or annoy me when I hear them talk." (I found that odd but whatever. I like beautiful, smart women.)

But you want to go beyond generalization and common fantasies, and stick to your beautiful dreams, while you stay true to your reality. In your beautiful dreams lies the person to help your dreams come true—to work on your projects; give you a hand when you fall; comfort you in your sorrow and sadness; be there when you least expect it; and love you forever for who you are. And you will respond in kind. If he or she doesn't come, you must go get him or her.

❏ Conquer the Love You Deserve

Conquering the love you deserve is a challenge that requires serious commitment and hard work—nothing that you don't have to dominate, but it would be a wise move to prepare well for the challenge. The question is this: where do you go to conquer the love you deserve?

Venues: The sky is the limit, but you must be true to the span of your wings and the power of your engines. Respect the capabilities of your aircraft, and be aware of all restricted and prohibited airspace. If you're living in poverty, rich boys and girls are out of your league. If you're poorly educated, high-class individuals are off limits. If you don't believe in God, churches and other venues of worship are not in your circles. If you are a drug addict or stuck on welfare with three children, your wings are broken, and your engines are sputtering. You have some serious work to do. Basically, you cannot go to a cranberry field to find banana trees.

Although your package sets up your venues and boundaries, you shouldn't feel bad if your package is almost empty. No one has a full package, and many of the people with the best packages have fallen short. Be in the open. Prioritize social activities, such as nightclubs, movies, cruises, and community events, that involve a diversity of ethnicity.

I would not suggest going to bars. Usually, we're there to forget someone fast or liberate ourselves from deadly stress and frustration. With that said, however, I know someone who picked a husband at a bar and lived happily ever after. I guess it is true that we can find love in a hopeless place. I just wouldn't bet on it, nor do I recommend it. Consider that the greater your package, the greater your chances of conquering what you deserve on high ground.

Regardless of what you have up your sleeve, you should do all you can to conquer the love you deserve. Empowering yourself is a strong card in your hands. From here, you can be sure that when your long-awaited party begins, you will be in for long nights of fun, forever and ever.

The Power of Communication

Another trait that distinguishes us from other animals is the ability to communicate verbally. It is a great tool to help us succeed on the journey of life. Unfortunately, most of us are poorly equipped in the world of communication. Many factors, such as education, culture, philosophy, and political regimes, are to blame for this. We might have grown up in a family that doesn't allow us to express our feelings, thoughts, and emotions freely. It might be more like a military style of life, where we aren't allowed to ask questions or give an opinion. This type of oppression inhibits children's ability to develop the power of communication. When the time comes that communication is necessary in the outside world, they are handicapped.

For example, in committed relationships, the poor level of education of both lovers can be the perfect recipe for bad communication, as both are skilled to talk trash and communicate little. When the level of education of the lovers is too far apart, good communication may not be around all the time. The communication oppression from childhood could show up in the form of dominance in arguments as a way to compensate for the loss of freedom of speech during childhood. The normal communication processes are no longer a peaceful way of conveying one's ideas to others and listening to their responses. It becomes all about, "You listen to me. I don't have to listen to you." The focus is on what to say next instead of listening to what is being said.

In close and personal relationships, almost as a rule, we play nice and "swallow the fish by the tail," as we want to have fun, with the hope that after we move in together, things will improve, and surprise, surprise—here it is! We go to bed together, wake up together in the morning, compromised to make this last "until death do us part." Everything's hot and intensely pleasurable, as it's supposed to be. We desire to hit it every day and night, in every corner of the house, on the couch, sofa, tub, chair, toilet seat, kitchen table, floor, porch, and in backyard, sometimes after hide-and-seek or a poker game. All can be done, now that our desires are set to soar freely. The sky is the limit but also a trap. If we indulge in the fun of the freedom, five years later we will battle animosity and act like strangers in bed because we didn't cement the foundation of our sexual relationship communication. We gradually give less to and demand more of our relationship.

Very often, "until death do us part" turns into "split after few years." Only good communication can sustain the "sky is the limit" in a relationship. Any relationship dominated by bad communication faces constant winter storms after severe heat waves, thus gravely affecting love and care, romance, and sexual adventures. Talk to your lover about every dream of yours and of both of you. Be supportive and the best adviser, as you must, and I would be surprised to hear your complaints about sexual dissatisfaction.

Honesty. Once you're willing to abide by the rules of honesty—one of the greatest ingredients of communication—both of you will be at ease with each other because you both know that both of you are working toward the glory of both of you, which will reflect in the success of each of you. Honesty enriches trust. Trust is a strong supporting beam of any relationship. And please take into consideration that trust doesn't mean the absolute truth and nothing but the absolute truth. A person who can't handle lies misses the fact that honest people lie to cover a mess that would otherwise become a catastrophe. Some individuals prefer not to know that you've lied, and others understand lies. Therefore, come clean after the fact to reinforce trust, and stop if it was counterproductive.

The truth is that every person is a sinner. People lie, and many individuals are liars. When lies are allowed to breathe, they choke, and when they are oppressed, they become empowered. It's complicated! With that said, truth is pure and clean. If you can rely on it unconditionally in your relationship, you are blessed, but keep an open mind and consider a small lie, inconsistent and stagnant, as harmless as it may be. You always have the choice.

Monkey See, Monkey Do—or Do Not. Human beings learn from the actions of others. Thus, follow the principles of couples with a communication hot dish. They have fun in bed, which is the very thing you want to happen in your bed too. The problem is, you must follow their principles on your own terms, or you'll be imitating someone's lifestyle. That would be counterproductive.

❏ The Castle on Top of the Hill

Every time you aim for excellence, you cherish success and happiness that others wish for. Make your relationship stand out by the power of its uniqueness. It doesn't need to be perfect; it doesn't need to be fake or flamboyant. It simply needs to be humble and real. Your castle on top of the hill is rich in friendship, laughter, jokes, and dirty talk. The bedroom is hot, even when the chill of the valley of death is an intruder.

A relationship is complicated itself because two distinct individuals decided to unite, live together, have sex, procreate, raise a family, and make dreams come true. Each partner must give some away for the sake of the relationship microsociety. This is not an easy thing to do. The biological construct of the individuals makes this obligation hard to fulfill, but it's necessary and rewarding. Don't fall behind. Overcome the obstacles to get joy, happiness, worthiness, pleasure, and sex. A thriving relationship that stands on firm ground has all the ingredients women and men need for a wonderful life.

Dirty Talk

Out-of-nowhere sex, or surprise sex, such as a one-night stand with someone new we've picked up at the shopping center, nightclub, or house party, gets only a small piece of the pie or nothing at all, as we're more concerned with doing a good job. Speaking your dirty mind could send the wrong message—a slut, faker, or both—although the clichés (gimme, hard, faster, feels good, make me come, please don't stop, I am coming, yes, more!) should be ready for use in any sexual activity. They are the low level of dirty talk but are capable of enhancing sexual excitement.

For other circumstances, dirty talk has phases that we should respect. In phase one—sexting, texting, and pictures—the louder your mouth, the better. You will make his or her naughty imagination go wild. This phase is the red carpet to pleasure in the bedroom, with trophies under the sheets.

Phase two is inside the house. Mixing romance with flirting and compliments, such as "You're wearing my favorite underwear," then whispering in her ear, "I will do my best to return the favor," is a good recipe. With that said, let's make a dish!

❑ **Outdoor Talk**

"I wanna have some fun."

"I am craving your big ___."

"Do you want another round tonight?"

"I might be open for business."

"I like that you look in my eyes when I'm inside you."

"I love to hear you moan while I'm going down on you."

"I want you so bad that I wish I had wings."

"What are you wearing?"

"I miss your sweet, juicy___."

"I miss your ___ so bad that I can't stop fantasizing."

"I have a surprise for you. When do you want it? Tonight?"

"What number are you thinking of?"

"I miss the weight of your big ___ on my lips!"

❑ **Bedroom Talk**

"Are you ready for your erotic exam?"

"You're looking delicious."

"I love it when you're naked."

"Touch yourself for me."

"Can I watch you masturbate?"

"What do you want me to do to you?"

"How can I get you off?"

"I can't wait to slide my _____ inside you."

"Tell me where you want me to touch you."

"How are you going to punish me?"

"I can't wait to see your lips around my ____."

"I love when you're in control."

"Get on top of me until you come."

"How fast do you think I can make you come?"

"Tonight, I want to make you come again and again."

"I'm going to make you wake up the neighbors."

"How hard do you want it tonight?"

"I want to strip you right now."

"I like it when I come inside you."

"I love it when we come together."

"I love watching us in the mirror."

❑ Under-the-Sheets Talk

"I wanna see how hard you can make me."

"Show me how bad you want me."

"I wanna come hard."

"Show me who's the boss."

"Make me go crazy."

"I want to taste you."

"Bend over for me."

"I wanna fill you up."

"How deep do you want it?"

"I want to kiss every inch of your body."

"I miss your ____ so bad."

"I love the way you smell."

"You are so wet and warm. I love it. Do you like it?"

"Is it good for you?"

❑ Close and Personal

"I can't wait to be inside you."

"That feels good."

"How horny are you?"

"Push your ass against my ____. I want to feel all of you."

"You like it, don't you?"

"____ me!"

"____ me hard."

"Gimme!"

"Don't stop!"

"Bite me!"

"Do you want me to make you come?"

"Where do you want me to come?"

"You look so delicious between my legs."

"Do you want me lick it?"

"Your tongue feels so good right there."

"Tease me until I beg you for it."

"I want your ___ so bad; I could spend all day inside you."

"Spread your legs for me."

"I want to feel how wet you are."

"Your ___ is mine tonight."

"Sit on my ___."

"If you keep it up, I'm gonna come."

"I am coming!"

❑ Derogatory Talk

"Be a good little ___, and spread your legs for me."

"___ me like a whore."

"___ the ___ out of my ___."

"Suck my ___."

"Smack my ass."

"___ me off."

❑ Complimentary Talk

"I love it when you suck my___."

"You have an amazing ___."

"You're so good at licking my ___."

"I like it when you bite me."

"Your ___ makes me hard every time."

"You look so sexy."

"Your ____ feels good against my ass."

"What a hot ass you have. It makes me want to ____."

"Your ____ feels good inside me."

"I like you in yoga pants. It makes me want to ____ you so bad."

"You smell like heaven. I could stay here all night."

"You taste deliciously sweet. I could eat you for every meal."

"I love hearing the sound of your ass slapping against me."

❑ The Anticipation Talk

"I'm going to smack it really good tonight."

"I'm going to come all over your body [in your mouth]."

"If you're nice to me I'll ____ your ____ [swallow/let you come inside me/all over my body] tonight."

"I can't wait to be inside you."

"If you'll be good, I'll reward you with a nice ____."

"All day, I've just been fantasizing about ____ your ____."

"When I'm done with you, you're not gonna feel your body."

❑ The Request Talk

"I want to lick your ___."
"I want no ___ tonight. Just lick my ___ right, all night long."
"Can we go wild and rough?"
"Masturbate for me. It makes me so horny."
"Let's play a sex game."
"I will do anything for a blow job."
"I wanna come inside you."

Make your special menu from this long list. Don't sacrifice yourself by memorizing a dirty-talk vocabulary list from here to China or talk dirty every day or every time you have sex. It will become meaningless, thus ineffective. Just a few words can serve you well—and only every now and then. Select the words that fill you. "Harder, faster, gimme, that feels good, rub my ___" may cut it. In any sexual acts, a short phrase, even one word, uttered with sincerity, feeling, and emotions, can seal the deal. Less can be more.

Beware of fake: if she's dry, ugly, has a small ass, or has a condition, or if he's skinny and below average, don't say, "I can't wait to taste your juicy vagina; you're the world. I am dying to smack your big, fat ass. Your vagina always smells sweet," or "I can't wait to touch your muscles. I feel you deep inside me." Whatever your intensions are, they may be taken as an insult. But you already know that.

Human beings are very fortunate to have ongoing innovations that improve every aspect of our lives. The first humans were born about two million years ago. We modern humans arrived about 200,000 years ago, and only about 70,000 years ago, the first speech sound was born. What an evolution revolution that sprinted us to excellence, while the other creatures crawled into evolution stagnation—another great gift that revolutionized the way we interact with one another and made communication as easy as drinking a glass of water.

Our jungle ancestors had sex too, but you can imagine that flirting by sign language; must've been laughable! But even our recent ancestors of 150 years ago had limited ways to flirt and talk dirty. With the invention of the telephone around 1876, we had another way to flirt and talk dirty, yet nothing compares to the power of the internet and smartphones. We hear, we see, we watch, we talk, we text, and we live video stream our wishes, desires, and actions. This latest communication gadget allows us to prepare the game field anytime we want. We can start a flirting journey from a distance, in different ways, and end it close and personal, with dirty talk.

Some naughty expressions that are easy to understand include the following:

- I can't wait to open your legs wide and devour your sweet vagina like a hungry lion.
- I am going to take you on your knees like an angry bear.
- I will fold you like a mannequin and give it to you until you beg for mercy.
- Your sweet pie is my dinner tonight.
- Tonight, I need a delicate downtown sweep.
- Enter gently and romp it your way.
- I am ovulating tonight.
- Rough is my game.

Sending your lover a picture of a cucumber or banana, followed by, "I am craving this," is easily understandable, and "Smack me hard; gimme; spread my ass; finger me" all have one meaning, but dirty talk is not a universal language. It's an individualized means for naughty communication, extracted from universal naughty language.

What makes me horny may turn you off, and not all terms and expressions arouse everyone in the same way. Sometimes the pleasure is so intense that we don't want to be disturbed with, "Is that good for you?"; "Can I smack your ass?"; "Let's change"; "Can I go harder?"

Dirty talk is distraction to some girls who need deep concentration to enjoy sex. I've heard, "Can you shut up and just fuck me?" To avoid trouble, settle dirty talk during the courtship or prior to getting down and dirty.

Since dirty talk arouses sexual desire and makes sex entertaining, enthusiastic, and pleasurable and galvanizes the relationship, everyone should have personalized dirty talk in their sexual repertoire. In addition to that, moaning, groaning, and screaming take the king's chair. Next to it sits "one-size-doesn't-fit-all." On this chair, we find individual likes and tastes. Determine what yours are, and make them your best friends forever. Never forget that anything straight from your soul is priceless. Don't ever hold yourself back, and don't apologize for your intense emotions. Explain later, if necessary.

29

The Party Has Begun

In our childhoods, we could think about the future and dream. We recognized limitations that were the product of age and inexperience, where freedom was limited, quarantined, and monitored. And that wasn't cool at all. We wanted to be out in the wild to experiment and make our dreams become reality, no matter how stupid or impossible they were in the eyes of the world.

One of the things that always bothered us was forced conformity. We were cool with some friends our parents had hooked us up with, but we hated how they shepherded us around, boys and girls. All that triggered our desire to grow fast and become men and women, to do what we wished, live wherever we want, have sex whenever we desired, and marry whoever we loved.

Whether or not this relates to you, from the time you started wondering about sex until you started living with someone, you were learning sex. Now, you're an adult in charge of your destiny, sharing the bed with someone to whom you gave something special and making a big compromise. You must soar with your sexuality, applying what you've learned and welcoming innovations to get the whole sexual pie. Yes, it's the party time, celebration of life, freedom, and sexual thrills you've long awaited!

❑ Enjoying the Party

The celebration of life in a relationship is like being in a restaurant. You've heard about it, chosen it, and picked a day to visit it. You couldn't wait for this day to come, and here you are. You look at the menu and choose what looks delicious from the pictures, or you read the menu and pick the most delicious picture in your brain. The greater the variety, the greater the chances of your satisfaction. What friends have recommended and what the people next to your table are eating can be a great help. And you'd better try different dishes every time you visit. So yes, now that you can go to bed and wake up with your lover every day, and you can have sex in every corner of your house as often as you want, take the opportunity to make your bedroom a special place for sex celebration. Here's a small helping hand:

The mastery. If you've done a good job in learning the ropes, you've read books and other sexual materials. Read more intensely now for mastery and discovery of new heights. If you haven't read, start eagerly because you have much to catch up.

The source. As sex begins in your brain, keep your

imagination alive. Also, watch porn as an inspirational learning source. To begin with, porn enriches your sexual position varieties, if you catch the catch. Don't position yourself exactly as you've seen the actors do—unless you're making a home video. Porn has the visual priority, which is main reason guys watch it more than girls.

To position yourself in such a way that his penis must be seen sliding back and forth into your vagina is important in porn, not in your bedroom—unless that is a turn-on for you. Don't be annoyed by what you know is an insult to your intelligence, such as taking a penis out of the anus and shoving it into her vagina (or worse yet, into her mouth). That's obviously a big pile of cow's manure; ignore it. Watch attentively the good work of the tongue on the penis or vagina. Homemade videos, especially those whose characters' faces are not shown, are real. They may inspire you—monkey see, monkey do—and fade your inhibition away.

Protection. A condom is a speed bump on the sexual road, which marriage eliminates but not entirely. Remember that the time to show what you can deliver sexually has come, so you should increase your use of condoms around and during her ovulation to reduce the risk of unwanted pregnancies. There are always consequences to unwanted pregnancy. This practice is recommended for all lovers.

To reduce the inconvenience or interruption of fun, put the condom on him yourself. It shows how much you care for yourself, and it shows cooperation and interest in making it fun and safe—and it keeps his arousal going by your touch. Or touch yourself and him while he puts it on himself.

Sex room. Couples who can afford a sex room have it. Sex toys belong there; special chairs and other furniture for sexual thrills belong there. They go there quite often to enjoy themselves without reservation or prejudice. This room is your Las Vegas. And don't forget: "What happens in Vegas stays in Vegas." Don't be fooled that now you can indulge in weed, drugs, alcohol, watching your phone, and "fuck like rabbits" on your terms, or in four to five years, sexual boredom will knock loudly.

Favorites. Whether or not you succeeded in mastering sex positions or types of sex, always choose your favorites for the endgame. Mix favorites every time, and sexual adventure will be glorious every time.

Homemade meals. It could be that learning sex is against the fundamental principles of your philosophy. If so, you can use your imagination, frequently and extensively, to enrich your menu within boundaries. Beware of God's messages delivered by men. There's always the possibility that men—sinners and liars—distorted God's message before delivering it to you. And men could bring penitence on you for the sins Jesus Christ has already redeemed for you. Live an honest, fair sexual life.

❏ Best Friends Forever

"Best friends forever" is one of the best preventions for separation or divorce and a strong and well-maintained track on which your wagon of relationship will travel throughout the country. That's not to say there won't be grit and rocks on the tracks, but they will be harmless.

Jennifer and Anthony united their two bodies into one soul when they were both twenty-one. They were not a perfect match; they didn't have love at first sight or an incredible passion for each other, but they managed to sail through rough waters just fine. Society graded their relationship as beautiful. Twelve years later, they separated. Friends couldn't believe it because "You two were so friendly!" Indeed, they were! Separation didn't kill their friendship, not ever. On the contrary, they became like brother and sister—unusual, but proof that when you treat your lover as your best friend, you can harvest the benefits forever. Instead of living by the nonsense that you finally have him or her all for yourself, your cooperation is under your command. Act as if you are still doing all that you can to turn him or her into a best friend with distinct, unmatchable qualities. Your lover is indeed all that and more. The wild bird you worked so hard to catch requires a special cage. Nurture it, or it will flee far from your sight.

30

The Party Is in Trouble

Life's trickeries can be stunning, but tragedy striking you with a divorce within six months after the wedding is a result of having learned the ropes poorly and/or ineffective application of the knowledge acquired. I am not a fan of the combination of zodiac as a mandatory check for a relationship's success. I know you could've put a ring on the right finger and then see ugly changes rise to nasty surprises soon after the wedding. Double is the trouble when the wrong lover is involved—if you like to have sex a lot, rough sometimes or most of the time; you are open to fantasy, such as threesome with two men and you; or you are open to swinging and group sex, a church guy is a wrong lover for you. Any guy who is extremely jealous and a control freak, who demands unconditional obedience in bed, is the wrong lover for you.

If you want a large family and he hates kids, he's the wrong partner for you. If you go on with the hope that your lover will change to your wishes, you might as well drink poison. The secret to a successful party lies in the ability of the lovers to adjust their attitudes to fit the conditions of the party and to be willing to alter the path of the river, if such becomes necessary.

Jasmine was going through wedding arrangements. It was fun to be around her, for she was charming, hot, open-minded, and fresh. She was always making us guys get an erection with her flirting and sexual imagination. She talked a lot about her sexual-adventure dreams after the wedding. "I'll be fucking in every corner of the house—on the kitchen counter, kitchen table, in the closet, on the porch, in the bathroom, on the stairs, everywhere," she told us. Whether or not she would practice those fantasies, her message was that once you're married, you earn the right to enjoy and explore your sexuality as you wish.

In less than a year, she got married. Six months later, she was divorced. It was a physical and emotional marital tragedy that was reflected in her rapid weight loss and her change of personality from energetic and happy-go-lucky to a quiet, conservative woman bearing some shame or trauma. Clearly, she didn't enjoy the party. She was a victim of a mismatch—the wrong partner, among other detrimental factors to a marriage, such as unwillingness to make big sacrifices to save a ship in great distress.

There are tons of obstacles on the marriage roads to glory. Putting a ring on the finger of the wrong partner is the worst mistake you can make and an obstacle almost impossible to overcome. Splitting up, separation, or divorce will be lurking, waiting for the best opportunity to strike. My friend's big dream—sex in every corner of the house—went down the drain way too soon. Many women travel along the same disappointing roads. Don't do that.

It doesn't matter how long you've been dating and how much sex you've had, the thrills of marriage last for about five to ten years, and then trouble starts its engine. The train begins its journey to destination chaos or hell. Stress and frustration begin pouring from everywhere. Employment, financial difficulties, the burden of raising a family, and life's nasty surprises (such as loss of employment, death of parents or family members, dreams and projects drifting away) are some of the unlisted conductors. They didn't even buy the tickets. They were lurking, we dropped our guard, and they jumped on board and took over. We aren't having much sex now, and when we do, it's not the same. The party sucks and is in trouble. The poor blame poverty, forgetting that superstars and rich people are always splitting up, separating, and divorcing and not always as publicity stunts. Trouble comes to neglected parties in all social classes.

It doesn't matter what you've done or not done. When your party is in trouble, your next step is to save it.

31

Saving the Party

Marriage is an all-night-long house party, except we can't just call the cops and plumbers to kick the intruders out and fix the water leaks. This party is different. The lovers are the organizers, bartenders, caterers, deejays, dancers, and security guards. Only we can bring back what made the party fun and enthusiastic. Love and romance and preventive measures are the best supporters.

❏ Love and Romance

There isn't any medicine more powerful than love and romance for saving a relationship, for the fact that we are products of love and romance. We are nurtured with love and grew up needing love and giving love. We are love. Women have and give it more than men. Whether or not we understand it, love is an affection we have for people we worship and/or want to stay close to. We love our parents like no one else, then our brothers and sisters, friends, teachers, coworkers, and idols. When puberty comes, we love those we feel sexually attracted to. Later, we'll love our soul mates dearly, followed by our children and stepchildren, who get just about all our love. (I wish there were some leftovers to be spread to humanity for peace, harmony, and brotherhood.)

Regardless of our feelings and interpretations of love, we are outcasts when our souls don't carry much love. We are lost when we're not loved. We're on pedestals when we're loved. Love is fundamental to our emotional balance, happiness, strength, and endurance. Another sure thing is that, to our shame, we haven't been giving love the seat it deserves. We have been letting it struggle with pain and suffering, only to see our emotional world spin in hatred and disarray, all the way down to lovers.

We plan and go to sleep, thinking about the best ways to make it work. We're focused on making a difference every day, whatever it takes, and that's wonderful. Love doesn't deserve any less attention. It sits close to the oxygen we need for our survival. If your heart is empty, there could be an emotional imbalance you must fix. Otherwise, the consequences can hit you at any time. It could be that they already have. Even beautiful girls, who should worry less about lack of love—somehow their hearts are filled with love from birth, and it never runs out—need to stay vigilant to many suckers, such as the decline of love and romance, pushing a straw deep into their hearts to suck dry the juices of love.

It seems that suddenly the world has become too much

of a macho man and is spinning way too fast for love and romance. And romance is not only gravely wounded but also left with the short end of the stick in the struggle to stay alive on the battlefield of love.

I hope I am wrong because sex is the ultimate thrill of life. Romance is the silky road of passionate sex. Either way, the more we understand and respect romance and sex, the greater the chances for our enjoyment of both. For that, focus your efforts on learning and evolving in love and romance, instead of priming yourself to be a sex master. It doesn't matter how hard you try; you won't master the game of sex because of its complexity and dependence on hundreds of factors. And romance (or lack of it) pretty much dictates the wealth or poverty of sex.

Romance is something you can exercise without boundaries. It flows freely through all people and cultures, and it's loved like chocolate. It actually beats chocolate in its goodness to the heart, mind, body, and spirit. In the end, love, romance, and sex are games like any other games. We cannot just take an empty seat at the table and play hard. We need to know the game inside and out and then practice, practice, and practice some more. And then continue to practice.

Educate yourself to the maximum extent, and be aware that, in this game, you will have a bad hand, a horrible hand, and a losing hand more often than you think—that's regardless of how much you know and understand. You'll have to stay focused on the better hands coming next. Life is a journey filled with a variety of joy from the very beginning to the end. The party is more exciting when love and romance are in the room. They make the room so hot that you have to take off your clothes. Don't let any chill make you wear another layer of clothing to protect your skin—that's to remind you that if you're a victim of sexual abuse, gather your strength, sink your traumas and regrets to the bottom of the ocean, and replace them with loving memories. And then indulge in love, romance, and sex— best friends for your party.

It doesn't matter how we twisted it. Sex is the only reason and the strongest beam of a relationship. Love comes second; personality and the means to provide come third. Any rich man or woman living without sex is empty. Therefore, once you care for the sex, love, and the means to provide, your party will be fun again. This trio is the band running the show under the sheets. You must feed each triplet the best nourishment you can afford. That could be novelties, out-of-ordinary sex, exotic vacations, frequents nights at motels and hotels, cruises, or whatever you can think of to bring back her desire to have sex with you again, and again, and always.

Family counselors and sex therapists are great caterers for your party, but you could do without them. At least, consider them as the last friends to save your party. It could be that all the party needs is more passionate sex—making love—and frequent and better tongue jobs on her downtown, and a rough party every now and then to remind her of her teenage years.

You need to feed the needs so your needs can be fed. Please don't be dumb! Fight hard and smart for your regular-basis sex and glory in bed. Those who thought they wouldn't have to worry about the milk because they bought the cow now buy milk every day; they didn't feed the cow.

❑ Preventive Measures

Nobody can go on without some setbacks—heated moments of senseless arguments—but we can take measures to prevent catastrophe and frequent visits of intruders. We boost the measures that brought the shine and fun to the party, and we monitor intruders that brought the party to its knees. An open mind to improvements, which include innovation and friendship, is welcome. We can take a bullet for our best friends, but somehow, we let ignorance and stupidity meddle in the affairs of our relationship. Let's not allow any intruders to poke our parties in any way, shape, or form. A great party is all we have.

Menopause

I didn't have a clear understanding of menopause until now, while working on this book. Menopause is popularized as an extensive period of tormenting personality changes that women go through, starting in middle age, forty-five years of age. That's not quite right. Menopause is the age a woman stops menstruating. Her ovaries no longer produce eggs. If it happens before age forty, it's called premature menopause; if happens between ages forty and forty-five, it's called early menopause. About 5 percent of women have early menopause naturally.

You reach menopause when you haven't had a period for twelve consecutive months. If you have your ovaries removed, you'll experience sudden menopause. After you haven't had a period for twelve consecutive months, you enter the postmenopausal stage—the storm is gone, and the calm has started settling down.

It's widely accepted that menopause is directly related

to the decreasing number of eggs a woman produces, but scientists aren't sure of the causes behind menopause.

Before you experience menopause, you'll go through a transitional period known as perimenopause, the real troublemaker. It's the time when the ovaries begin to gradually make less estrogen, and the menstrual cycle gradually shortens until you no longer menstruate— menopause. Perimenopause usually starts in a woman's forties or even as early as her twenties.

The average length of perimenopause is four years, but for some women, this transition may last only a few months or continue for ten years or more. Perimenopause causes many physical and physiological changes, such as considerable weight gain, thinning of hair, less fullness of breasts, and brain and hormones modifications. You can have your period ten days or 120 days after your previous one. It's sometimes spotting and other times a geyser.

Sex in perimenopause is disturbed. Prepare yourself, wear gloves, and enter the ring with confidence—"To have a plan is to have the battle half fought." You may be lucky and have an easy fight. The common sexual symptoms of perimenopause are a decrease in estrogen, leading to a decrease in blood supply to the vagina and vulva, less collagen in the vulvar tissue, and changes in vaginal pH. These symptoms lower your sexual desire. You may notice that your pubic hair is thinning, your labia appear looser, and that your vulva and vagina have become drier, due to less fat. Headaches, mood swings, night sweats, and hot flashes are also common. These symptoms come in different degrees to different women, and no two women respond to them in the same way. With that said, there are common practices for dealing with the sexual symptoms during this transitional period to menopause.

"Use it, or lose it!" As you age, your vagina can become shorter, narrower, and less elastic, making intercourse uncomfortable. Continuous sexual activity can help prevent such changes. Masturbation comes in handy, as it's a solo play on your own terms.

Use lube. As you age, your natural lubrication decreases. Sex may be uncomfortable or even painful.

Kegel exercise. This is to strengthen your pelvic floor muscles, which participate in the muscle contractions during orgasm. Due to other related benefits, Kegel exercise is recommended for younger ages and after childbirth.

Unless you've neglected your life throughout the years, your health and sexuality should be in good condition. You know your body, your sexual power, and your capability. You know what you like and don't like. You know your favorite sexual positions, touches, and spots. You know the duration of the stimulation of your treasured land that you need. You know how to adjust yourself for the best touch, caress, and licks. You know how to best receive and give.

Now, more than never, you must exercise your sexual authority over your lover—nicely. You are navigating rough waters that he can't understand. He is the second in charge under your command. Be smart and demand cooperation. Don't take this opportunity to put your lover on a sex diet, what others call "vagina strike," or you too will suffer, especially if sexual dissatisfaction opens the doors for cheating.

There are plenty of medications, doctors, pharmacists, and advice from friends to help you sail and enjoy sex on the perimenopause roller coaster, which fades away after menopause.

If You'd Known Then
What You Know Now

I found myself frequently visited by the bitterness of a regretful adventure that happened forty-three years ago. I was a high school senior, waiting impatiently for a girl to put out the flames of my crash to my crush Maria John (to learn the details, read the chapter on confidence in my first book, *Stay Ahead of the Game*.) Brenda Emilia did exactly that, except more powerfully; she crushed me with love at first sight in her freshman year. Like Maria John, she was out of my league, but my heart didn't care. I later discovered who Brenda's family was, and I pictured myself as part of that and the future of our family. I had doubts sometimes about becoming her boyfriend, but I always saw myself as capable of having anyone. When I found out she was the best friend of my schoolmate, I saw the light in the middle of the tunnel.

Soon after, I had a weekend-and-holidays job as a

security guard in a government building that was, to my surprise, on the street where they lived. That was the light at the end of the tunnel. I could see the two most important people in my life at the time, going for walks, to movies, or shopping on the weekends and holidays.

I did all I could to make sure she knew I was madly in love with her. I used her friend as bait. I continuously and deliberately approached them when they were together, proud to give Brenda opportunities to know that her best friend was my friend and schoolmate.

After I graduated and moved on to employment, I did my best to be at the high school to see her and say hello, yet I was afraid of telling her how madly in love I was with her. I didn't even ask my friend to hook us up because I was giving time for us to be good friends. That was the kind of idiot I was! In fact, to this this day, the popular advice is, "Do not to be friends with a person you're interested in."

At the office, three females coworkers and I had had become great friends with secrets. One of our secrets was "2x2," which stood for *secret crush*. They all knew Brenda, my 2x2. They told me she was dating, but it didn't bother me.

I finally gathered enough courage and asked Brenda to be mine. She declined, saying that she had a boyfriend. I was persistent, as if she was lying to me. I had not planned for a *no* as an answer. The adventure went from bad, to very bad, to a disaster. Thanks to my stupidity and immaturity, we went our separate ways, and she never talked to me again.

I lost her friendship and all possibility of making my heart happy.

Despite my moving on, she remained in my dreams. I couldn't stop thinking of her. She sat very securely in my heart. I knew this because when I immigrated to the United States of America, I asked my girlfriend in Cape Verde to bring my writings with her. She said, "I only found poems and things about Brenda. You never fell in love with me." Since my irresistible passion for Brenda wasn't a surprise to her, she added, "I am just kidding. I know you love me, and you had a crush on her before I met you."

Some events of the past cut us deeply in our hearts and remain like strong, burning charcoal under the ashes. Increase the layers of the ashes to stay warm and comfy with the lovers you have now.

What affects us greatly when we age is the increasing female sexualization that we face. We're aware that girls depicted in the media and hip-hop videos, for example, are meant to arouse boys (and men) before female freedom of expression and sexual empowerment. They make old men cry or wish they were young again. A friend in his sixties said to me, about twelve years ago, "Where were all the girls in my day?" He came down to earth and answered his own question, saying, "They were there. I just didn't see them. The sexualization of girls has become so bizarre [that] the female characters on video games are better looking than the real ones walking on the streets."

"Sex sells" is no bullshit. Instagram and all other online platforms where pictures and videos are shared add salt to middle-aged men's wounded hearts. I assume it's the same for women. We feel like winners who didn't make the cut. Regret never leaves us.

There's the other side of the river, where *if-you'd-known-then-what-you-know-now* behaves differently. Here lies all the great memories we cherished with lovers—or even with that one-night stand—bringing smiles to our faces and joy to our hearts when we remember the fun. On the other hand are disturbing feelings when we think about things we could've done with a person when we had the chance—bittersweet feelings that refuse to leave us alone! Due to inexperience, ignorance, or arrogance of youth, we didn't bother to explore, and appreciate what we had. Now we know that humans will lose their beauty, strength, and endurance; that after giving birth, a woman's breasts are less firm, and her vagina can become dry over time; that women will go through a sea of factors that interfere with their sexuality; and that physical decline and illness can hinder our lovers' ability to do what we want, and we recall the opportunities we had to appreciate a girl but didn't.

If you have been there and have done it—well or poorly—you know that everyone has bittersweet feelings and regrets as a product of ignorance, neglect, or fear. Life is very complex and demanding, and sometimes it strikes us unmercifully. As a social beings and creatures endowed with the ability to have sex—one of the most powerful acts—it's almost impossible to escape bittersweet feelings or regrets related to relationships. There were too many cards on the table, and sharp, pointed objects were everywhere, poking our sexual fun, which, apparently, we didn't notice, or we wouldn't be complaining.

Of course, it hurts that you were dying to have him inside you or be inside her just one more time; to spend just one night with him or her. You can't stand that she got married and made dreams you two talked about. She's getting it every night while you bounce from relationship to relationship, and you've gone months without the touch of a woman and the scent of a vagina. Since you can't change history, but you can build a future with what you have, love your woman, and appreciate her as she is. Explore what you haven't explored to make her feel special. Show your passion, compassion, and appreciation. Let go of what you fought for but didn't get, or you will be living with a ghost. No one is a full package. The more you linger on the taunting illusion of the past, the more you hinder the chances of your living longer, happier, and healthier. This principle applies to women too.

If you're young, please review chapter 6, "Learning What You'll Know Later," to recall what causes trouble in middle age, and avoid them because it will be worthwhile. If you've done well, whips of the past have spared you. If you're a victim of sexual trauma, whether you're young or old, the following approach may help: regardless of how well you managed your love and sexuality, you can't go on, bonded to selfishness and disregarding the principles of relationships and life. There are obstacles on the road that you must overcome. You are standing here due to whatever happened to you, both good and bad, because you have wishes and desires, and God has a plan.

For the most part, our actions in the past were driven by our best decisions and abilities at the time. Don't linger over thinking, *If I'd known then what I know now.* You have the present to live, the future to build, and sexual needs to attend.

34

Erectile Dysfunction

Many phenomena of life force themselves in and stay, giving us no choice but to make room for them and to embrace the chills and bitterness they bring along. Erectile dysfunction, or impotence, is one such phenomenon. Yet, as sad as it sounds and as troublesome as it is, erectile dysfunction is part of the aging process. Like wrinkled skin, gray hair, decreased mobility, and visual decline, everybody will suffer from erectile dysfunction in some way, mild in some and severe in others. Statistics say that about 40 percent of men will suffer erectile dysfunction after middle age, and all men will be touched by it at some point. It's estimated there are more than three million cases in the United States each year.

Erectile dysfunction is defined as, "Inability of a man to have or keep an erection firm enough for a satisfying sexual activity." Erectile dysfunction is men's worst enemy, an ugly monster in the bedroom and a nightmare under the sheets. It causes stress, frustration, low self-steam, and strain to relationships. It shouldn't be such, but it is because humans allow psychological fear to interfere with their sexual pride—the macho. Any time we have sex, the performance evaluation in the backs of our minds shifts to high gear. We forget the numerous factors that contribute to our less-than-usual sexual performance or that of our partners. If we don't have clues to her satisfaction and orgasm, we are conditioned to ask, "Did you come?"

Some generous lovers lie to make us feel macho or to unload our heavy burden. A tight hug and a sweet kiss relieve us, but not all women are generous. Those who aren't make matters worse, even at times when they are the contributing factor. They may show anger and frustration over our poor performance or lack of performance. And they don't know that just a few dirty words can bring a man's penis from zero to one-hundred power in five seconds or less.

In no time, an inferiority complex covers you from head to toe, and sporadic misses become a dysfunction. Heavy alcohol consumption, cardiovascular disease, and diabetes are the main culprits, regardless of gender.

In aged relationships, love, passion, and desire, free will, understanding, and cooperation push impotence to the living room or kitchen and keep the erection under the sheets, in both of you.

The female erectile dysfunction is less publicized because women can hide it, but women do suffer libido decline, as do men. If she's a good faker, she blinds a man. That's a very bad strategy with consequences, but who am I to stop tragedy? Numerous men want their women to be horny every day and act actively the same, every time they have a party. When there is a dip in enthusiasm and participation, they complain instead of understanding and cooperating, which are two of the first responders to erection for both men and women. Medication and other treatments are next.

Sex is a pleasurable activity that requires an erect penis only when a woman is yearning for intercourse. Remember, there is more than one way to skin a cat. A smart and willing lover can get what she wants from her man at any age. Erectile dysfunction does diminish the intensity of the party, but it is not a death sentence to sexual pleasure. And it usually hits when our sexual needs are, in general, greatly reduced.

Whether man or woman, you may be the only one to blame for your sexual predicament. Your health condition and lifestyle can pretty much determine whether your sexuality will be hit with a brick or pulled by an angel to a smooth sail throughout your life. Get with the program, faithfully. For every man's illness or sickness, God created a plant right next to it and allowed doctors, nurses, and hospitals to be there. A man can push stupidity aside, get up, dust himself off, correct his mistakes, and repair his behavior. Do you see any excuses? I don't.

35

The Endgame

The endgame comes in different shapes and forms for different people and couples and is mostly determined by health. Some people never lose what it takes to have sex, while others start experiencing libido decline or even give up sex in menopause. If you've taken good care of your heart and health—plenty of sex, love, care, harmony, exercise, and diet—you'll not be affected much or at all during the endgame. If, however, you neglected your heart with resentment and hatred toward men or women, and you smoked, abused drugs and alcohol, or lived a frustrating life, you will face libido decline and mobility restriction, and you will battle health complications from years of neglect. The chances are your endgame will be messy, regretful, and painful.

I heard of a couple in their early seventies who gave up sex due to poor communication, lack of harmony, and free will, and I assume erectile dysfunction was the primary suspect, as it usually is. How bizarre! Also, wishing death from the bottom of your heart to your lover, who you now see as someone obstructing your advancement, would be a big pile of stupidity on your doorsteps.

During the endgame, it is sad to see any relationship doomed to hell by the lack of understanding, love, care, and sex, since the endgame is the play for aged and old couples in aged relationships, where both partners know each other inside and out—what pleases and what brings anger and madness. There shouldn't be surprises. Now is the time to use the wisdom of experience to your advantage.

At seventy years of age, you can't take on an exhilarating approach to your sexual enjoyment. Your physical and physiological conditions don't allow you to deliver astonishing novelty or any demanding sexual activities. Stand-up sex, rough, and kinky aren't on the menu anymore, nor will they ever be. That time is gone. However, you can master some things that youngsters (possibly you, too, at that age) pay poor attention to: oral sex, especially cunnilingus, and appreciation of what you have in every possible way. Don't decrease your love and care for your lover as the years go by. Do the opposite. And never forget sex.

Sex is an endeavor of such a great amplitude, and we can take benefit of it until we die. On top of that, we have the advancement of medical science on our sides. Understand your physical and physiological limitations. Try to go over or cope with them to the benefit of your relationship and sexuality. If there's a will, there's a way. That's all. Besides, what is more important that you would be doing here? I see not much. And it's a shame to be a loser in relationships and an embarrassment in sexuality during the endgame.

If your endgame finds you lonely, clean up that mess and move on. I've heard of people in nursing homes who got married at the age of ninety-seven, for whatever it was worth it. This leaves you with no excuses for not having sex when you're old, unless you chose so. However, don't force yourself to be the exception to the rule. Simply play the game until the game is over.

Afterword

There is no doubt we'll never understand nature, biology, and God's plan, vision, work, and purpose. What we're sure of is that we humans are blessed with sexual enjoyment that no other creatures can match. Any sexual enjoyment that other animals have is just a drop in the ocean of human sexual thrill. So much so that noble evolution and revolution had stagnated when we modern humans arrived, about 200,000 years ago. From there, we took the route of developing and enhancing what's in us and discovering ways to live better and enjoy sex like no other creatures.

To honor the winners, heroes at birth, born for the continuity and difference that we are, and to carry the torches of hope and prosperity to those before us, for us, and to those after us, we must reproduce, and most importantly, we must have a great sexual journey. This mission requires sacrifices, which we recognized early and attempted to get away from. You might recall that when we were young, we didn't want to grow up. Other times, we couldn't wait to grow up and have more and different kinds of fun. We battled puberty, had lovers, and started having sex. When the boat started rocking, we jumped in the water for safety, or so we thought. We noticed our mistake as we started sinking alone.

We looked forward to having a lover again to have sex on a regular basis. A relationship gives that, in return for personality, education, integrity, and wealth. The right partner and matching partners are important but not even closely necessary as relationship maintenance. Love at first sight is a great head start and gives an outstanding contribution to the love castle, but that will not withstand the winds of relationships without nurture and proper nutrition. Venerating the same philosophical principles, political views, religious practices, culture, and traditions favors the relationship and sustains sexual satisfaction under proper maintenance. If you face differences in your relationship, you face more demanding maintenance, yet it's doable, and you should pay the price. It's worthwhile.

From love, passion, and sex we came to become passionate, loving, caring, and procreators. Through sex, the most powerful human act (which I don't tire of reminding you), we discovered the real wonders of life. We, the humans, are the chosen ones, endowed with the ability to enjoy it like no others. Let's honor our sexuality to the best of our capabilities, without prejudice, through continuous learning and the application of knowledge.

Until we meet again, indulge in the utmost thrill of life—sex.

Author's Note

I have realized that we get entangled with the obligations of life, which become continuously more demanding, resulting in our poor attention to our sexual lives. If that is not bad already, we don't have consistency of attention. Sexual dissatisfaction is a sneaky issue through all classes and group ages, and I believe this is a worldwide phenomenon. It's sneaky because it has power to cause a variety of social and health complications without disturbing our lives significantly. It's like a delicious meal we should have on a regular basis, but we shrug it off because if we don't have it, we'll still do fine. This is a bad philosophical principle that we should tackle ferociously! It's a mistake to leave sex in the dark, on the nonpriority list.

The number of us who are having unsatisfactory sex life is mindboggling, and that's the reason I got drawn into writing this book. It's a mission from God, and I am glad I dearly accepted it, not only because it should help you improve your sex life, but it also enriched my experience and knowledge to illumination.

Let's reflect on the fact that we take many drugs to fix problems caused by insufficient sex, such as stress, frustration, depression, anger, and madness, while having sex will fix and prevent such ailments from occurring. It is not by chance that sex is the most powerful act and the greatest pleasure granted to us. It's my sincere hope that the information and psychology in this book serve you in the same manner they served me.

Let's honor sex by indulging in its greatness!

Acknowledgements

I thank God for the wit, grit, and wisdom I needed to write this book. I thank my mom and dad for life, nurturing, support, and inspiration. I thank sons, fans, and readers, particularly those who have encouraged me to go on, including my niece Thelma, my greatest challenger and inspiration.

Printed in the United States
by Baker & Taylor Publisher Services

Printed in the United States
by Baker & Taylor Publisher Services